Remembering
CAMBODIA

Remembering
CAMBODIA

Photography by ROBERT JAMES ELLIOTT
Text by STEFAN SMITH

© 2013 Marshall Cavendish International (Asia) Pte Ltd

First published in 2002 by Times Editions, reprinted 2003, 2006, 2007, 2008
This paperback edition published in 2013 by Marshall Cavendish Editions
An imprint of Marshall Cavendish International
1 New Industrial Road, Singapore 536196

All rights reserved

No part of this publication may be reproduced, stored in a retrieval system or transmitted, in any form or by any means, electronic, mechanical, photocopying, recording or otherwise, without the prior permission of the copyright owner. Requests for permission should be addressed to the Publisher, Marshall Cavendish International (Asia) Private Limited, 1 New Industrial Road, Singapore 536196. Tel: (65) 6213 9300, Fax: (65) 6285 4871. E-mail: genref@sg.marshallcavendish.com

The publisher makes no representation or warranties with respect to the contents of this book, and specifically disclaims any implied warranties or merchantability or fitness for any particular purpose, and shall in no events be liable for any loss of profit or any other commercial damage, including but not limited to special, incidental, consequential, or other damages.

Other Marshall Cavendish Offices:
Marshall Cavendish Corporation. 99 White Plains Road, Tarrytown NY 10591-9001, USA • Marshall Cavendish International (Thailand) Co Ltd. 253 Asoke, 12th Flr, Sukhumvit 21 Road, Klongtoey Nua, Wattana, Bangkok 10110, Thailand • Marshall Cavendish (Malaysia) Sdn Bhd, Times Subang, Lot 46, Subang Hi-Tech Industrial Park, Batu Tiga, 40000 Shah Alam, Selangor Darul Ehsan, Malaysia.

Marshall Cavendish is a trademark of Times Publishing Limited

National Library Board, Singapore Cataloguing-in-Publication Data
Elliott, Robert James.
Remembering Cambodia / photography by Robert James Elliott ;
text by Stefan Smith. – Singapore : Marshall Cavendish Editions, 2013.
p. cm.
ISBN : 978-981-4398-21-3 (pbk.)

1. Cambodia – Pictorial works.   2. Cambodia – Description and travel.
3. Cambodia – Social life and customs – Pictorial works   I. Title.

DS554.3
959.6 — dc23   OCN824825748

Printed in Singapore by Fabulous Printers Pte Ltd

Previous page: A face of a thousand stories —
a cyclo driver adjusts his krama.

Right: Enjoying the piece of walking along the water's edge at a fishing village north of Phnom Penh

CONTENTS

ACKNOWLEDGMENTS *9*

FOREWORD *11*

INTRODUCTION *13*

RELIGION *17*

PEOPLE *33*

CULTURE *61*

THE ECONOMY *69*

ON THE STREETS *99*

THE FUTURE *117*

ACKNOWLEDGMENTS

An unquestionable supportive role by my wife, Glenda, has allowed me to pursue my hobby, work, and passion for photography. Glenda's flexibility and encouragement has been reassuring and without it this book would not have been possible.

To my mum and dad (who is now passed away) for being such loving parents and giving me every opportunity to get a reasonable start in life, sometimes at their expense of going without.

To Agence France-Presse for granting me permission to use pictures I produced for, or on behalf of, AFP while I was a contract stringer in Cambodia. Unless stated, the photographs in this book were taken in and around the Cambodian capital Phnom Penh.

To my friend and colleague Stefan Smith, who didn't hesitate in taking up the challenge of producing the text for this book. His profound words and knowledge on Cambodia give the book insight and balance.

To my many colleagues and friends, too numerous to individualize, who have been encouraging in their persistent queries as to "how's the book going?" and "when will it be published?"

And finally, to the thousands of men, women, and children of Cambodia, who I have photographed over the past decade, for allowing me a glimpse into their lives — an ongoing struggle for survival.

— *Robert James Elliott*

Previous pages: Two children glide their boat across the calm waters of a lily pond.

Left: A cyclo driver transports a mother and son, and their precious possession — a painting of the Angkor Wat temple complex.

Following page: Putting the final artistic touches to a cement elephant.

FOREWORD

Cambodia's publicity over the past two decades has featured two main components — Pol Pot and the Khmer Rouge.

At the pinnacle of their destructive pursuit of Pol Pot's dream to create an agrarian utopia, the Khmer Rouge killed at least a million innocent men, women, and children.

Since the death of Pol Pot, and the defection of a majority of the Khmer Rouge rebels, Cambodia certainly projects a slightly different environment today.

There are still daily shootings, stabbings, robberies, and violence, but it is proportionally less in comparison to some other more developed countries.

It has to be remembered that conflict in the past was a way of life and was almost always settled with a gun or a grenade, so tradition takes time to change.

I recall an incident in 1998, in a village just south of the capital Phnom Penh, when what started as a couple of neighborhood children quarreling over something petty, escalated into senseless death. The mothers of the children got involved and started arguing; their fathers then resolved the situation by one of them producing a grenade that detonated. Three adults ended up dead, two with their heads blown off, and one father's brains splattered up a coconut tree.

Almost every person you meet in Cambodia has in some way been affected by conflict, violence, and certainly the trauma associated with its bloody, genocidal past.

Cambodia's real salvation will come with the influx of millions of tourists, who, up until now, have been semi-reluctant to visit the war-torn country in fear of their safety.

Angkor Wat, the temple ruins sitting in the north of the country at Siem Reap, is the real draw card and already attracts a number of international visitors, who fly there direct from Bangkok in nearby Thailand. This trickle of visitors will turn into a flood once the word is out about the real beauty of Cambodia and the friendliness of its people.

Steep in traditional mystique and religious beliefs, the country continues to display a very unique atmosphere — the smell of burning incense, the traditional sounds of Khmer music, as well as the monks chanting at Buddhist ceremonies. It is all intriguing and educational.

At a pagoda, children perform their traditional Khmer dances with pride and precision after months, and sometimes years, of training. The colorful performers, dressed in their detailed costumes, view dancing in public as a great honor.

Fishermen, who have been in their boats on the rivers for most of the night, arrive at the shores to unload their catches early in the morning. The fish are quickly loaded into cane baskets and whisked off to the markets.

On the outskirts of the capital, a woman struggles with a team of water buffalo pulling a plow through a small paddy field in preparation for planting. Within a week, she will return to do the backbreaking work of planting the rice seedlings and return months later for the harvest.

Women seem to be the predominant workers in Cambodia: in the home looking after children; in the fields plowing, planting, and harvesting the rice; in the streets with their stalls; and in the markets selling produce.

One can only be enthralled at the fascinating and unusual sights in Cambodia. It is a diverse country with charming people previously torn apart mentally and physically, but who continue to survive and will only get stronger. Cambodia is unique — there's nothing else like it.

— *Robert James Elliott*
November 2001

INTRODUCTION

Step into Cambodia and it is a world of smiles, where visitors can quickly develop the image of an idyllic, antiquated, and unhurried country of mystical jungle temples and Buddhist serenity. But behind the Khmer smile is a history of almost constant warfare.

Emerging from its past glories and modern tragedies, Cambodia is back among the international community, back on the tourist trail, and back on the map. With the Cold War over, it is longer ranked among pariah states, as it once was as a downtrodden and brutally violent part of both the Soviet and Chinese communist blocs. Now, donors and diplomats eager to guard or extend their Southeast Asian spheres of influence court it. Well-heeled tourists and backpackers alike are plying its temples, its beaches, its markets, and its bars. Entrepreneurs are busy working its rubber plantations and forests, foreign dignitaries its palaces and corridors of power.

For many among the Cambodian people, however, it is a thin veneer. Despite purveying an image of renewed normality behind their characteristic broad smiles that greet the visitor, the country cannot escape its recent past of having suffered what can certainly be classed as one of the most disastrous events in modern history — the Khmer Rouge revolution. It is a disaster that many are still struggling to come to terms with today.

Of all the turmoil of the twentieth century, there was probably no other reign that so totally and brutally altered the lives of an entire population. The events capped a thousand-year-long decline in the fortunes of the people of Cambodia — the diminutive successors to a once-mighty Khmer empire that spanned much of what are now Vietnam, Laos, and Thailand.

Archaeologists have traced Cambodia's roots back to early communities that existed on fish and rice, and lived in homes built on stilts, as many still do now. From the first to sixth centuries A.D., Cambodia was a part of the Funan kingdom, a time when the Khmer people began to develop outside trade, institutions, and a cultural expression and script heavily influenced by Indian Hinduism. But it was the era of the Angkorian empire — from the eighth to thirteenth centuries — that marked the pinnacle of Khmer civilization, still visible today in the Angkor temples and string of monuments that in recent centuries have been cut out of their jungle hiding places. Such was the Khmer power in that era, the image of the Angkor Wat temple is seen everywhere today, including the national flag. It is a vivid symbol of a power that once dominated its neighbors — Thailand and Vietnam.

The Thais sacked Angkor in 1431 after years of invasions and sieges, effectively marking the end of the Khmer empire. Then came a period of weak kings and internal civil disputes, successive invasions from Thailand and Vietnam, and European colonialism: the Portuguese and Spanish at first, and then as a colony of France in 1863 — which effectively saved Cambodia from being swallowed up by it neighbors. In

1941, the French installed nineteen-year-old Prince Norodom Sihanouk on the throne, in the belief that their colony was safe in his hands, while they tended to more pressing matters in Europe and elsewhere in their Indochina empire. But while the French historians of the time had looked down on the Khmer people as diminutive and even "lazy" subjects, the Westernization they brought also delivered a stronger sense of national identity for Cambodia. French colonial power was on the wane, and Sihanouk was an ambitious politician. Complete Cambodian independence was proclaimed in 1953, and Sihanouk stepped in to become the new figurehead and central player, in what was increasingly becoming a turbulent local political scene.

Cambodia's brief period of independence, today proclaimed by some (especially King Sihanouk) as the country's heyday, was short-lived. The country was doomed to become a victim of the war in Vietnam, which it had been seeking so desperately to keep out of. In 1969, the United States began carpet-bombing communist bases in Cambodia, killing tens of thousands of civilians and dragging another unwilling country into their war against communism. U.S. troops became active in Cambodia's jungles and paddy fields, as did the CIA. Considered too pro-communist, Sihanouk was ousted by a coup in 1970, sending him — and much of the country — into the arms of the Khmer Rouge ("Red Khmers"). Washington's proxy military government fought a losing battle up to 1975, and as the United States abandoned Indochina, the Khmer Rouge marched into Phnom Penh.

The waving crowds who lined the streets of Phnom Penh were quickly in for a shock. Almost overnight, entire cities were emptied, private property was abolished, and money became worthless. Families were torn apart as the new regime suddenly dictated that the entire country should become farmers, and guinea pigs for an unprecedented experiment in establishing an agrarian, communist utopia. This ideal was hammered out in the minds of the rebels' Paris Left Bank-educated leadership, and imposed by the largely illiterate, ruthless foot soldiers, who had little sympathy for the urban elite — who came to be know as the "new people" they had "liberated." Thousands who gave the slightest resistance were executed; some for crimes as simple as wearing a pair of glasses or speaking a foreign language — a symbol of Cambodia's bourgeoisie that the new rulers wanted to destroy. Cambodia became Democratic Kampuchea, a nation of slaves. It retreated into genocide as the outside world, in effect, closed its eyes.

As communists eager to cut themselves off from Western imperialism, the Khmer Rouge may have been seen as the natural allies of Vietnam, but their allegiances with their main sponsor, China, meant that for Soviet-bloc Hanoi, traditional rivalry came before ideology. After months of border clashes between the two communist states, Vietnam launched a full-scale invasion of Cambodia in 1978. Only then did the full horrors of Pol Pot's "Killing Fields" — as they came to be known thanks to the Oscar winning film — come to light. Disease, starvation, and Khmer Rouge torture or execution killed an estimated 1.7 million people — nearly a third of the population. Few Cambodians alive today — from King Sihanouk, to a peasant in the paddy field — escaped the bloodshed. Most lost close family members and all bear the scars. Furthermore, most of those who died were the country's educated elite, the very people who could rebuild the country. Others fled to the Cambodian Diaspora living in the United States, France, or elsewhere.

But despite their record of genocide, the ousted Khmer Rouge did not go away. On the contrary, they capitalized on a Western fear of Vietnamese communist expansionism, retreating to the hospitality of the Thai border and reaping fresh supplies, aid, and arms for their guerrilla war against Vietnam's ten-year occupation and puppet regime in Phnom Penh. Concern over their bloody wake was buried as Cold War allegiances — such as the U.S. détente with China — set the agenda. Vietnam's client government was isolated and unrecognized, and Vietnamese forces eventually pulled out in 1989 as Soviet power was on the decline. The international community stepped in with United Nations-sponsored elections in 1993, and Sihanouk was restored to the throne.

The government was a shaky coalition of ex-Vietnamese-backed puppet politicians and exiled royals. The Khmer Rouge, which boycotted the polls (after being allowed to participate), was formally outlawed in 1994. But the issue of how to deal with the Khmer Rouge sparked a bloody split in the fragile coalition government, which exploded in 1997 at the expense of the royalist party of Prime Minister Norodom Ranariddh — the son of King Sihanouk. Seeking to dismember the rebels, the government sought to encourage defections. But the mistrust on how this was handled gave government factions the opportunity to fight out their grievances once and for all. Eventually it was Prince Ranariddh who was ousted, and Hun Sen — a former Khmer Rouge commander who defected to Vietnam in 1977 — took charge. Ranariddh returned a year later for fresh elections, but appeared to have accepted his defeat, and some argued he appeared to be more involved in lining himself up for his ailing father's job.

Pol Pot died in 1998, and by the end of the century his henchmen were either in jail, in retirement, or dead. But as many rebel cadre found their way into the ruling ranks of the new Kingdom of Cambodia, the country has been left facing a painful dilemma. It is a question of whether to reopen old wounds and threaten a precarious infant state, or whether to finally deliver justice for the Cambodian people. The country has yet to find the answer, as it struggles to find its feet, emerge from poverty, and make its current, fragile peace — its first in over thirty years — last.

It is in the midst of this transition period where these following images find the country. It is a fragile and meager existence for many. This is a young population seeking out a life in the wake of catastrophe for their culture, religion, and economy. The economy has been shattered and is almost entirely dependent on foreign aid. Its traditional powerbrokers — the United States, Vietnam, Thailand, and France — are still jockeying for influence. Millions of land mines litter the countryside, ready to rip the limb or life from anyone seeking to exploit a rare piece of dry land. For those who have taken to the sex trade as a money-earner, the explosion of AIDS has proved equally deadly. Cambodia is still struggling to make ends meet, protect its culture from outside invaders, yet at the same time assimilate enough to survive and avoid once again being placed under foreign domination. It is a country that is trying to embrace its past, yet distance itself from it. In every scene and behind every smile Cambodia's continued battle for survival is glaring.

Previous page: Two young hawkers walk by the roadside carrying their poles of brightly colored plastic flowers.

RELIGION

Above: A girl places incense sticks in the welcoming hand of a temple Buddha.

Left: Novice monks share a joke during a break between their studies.

Theravada Buddhism is the dominant religion and is still in the throes of a major grassroots revival. It is a brand of Buddhism heavy in ritual, wide on tolerance, and thin on dogma — a branch often referred to as the "little vehicle" of Buddhist thought; which goes some way to explaining why a monk puffing on a cigarette is not an uncommon sight. Furthermore, national symbols, as well as animism, deep-rooted superstitions, and spirit worship are mixed in for good measure, while Hindu influences are still strong. In nearly all parts of the country, community life is centered on the pagoda.

The sight of monks draped in saffron robes provides a powerful, almost reassuring presence for Cambodians. Giving them daily alms adds to a key part of Buddhist philosophy — bringing merit to the donor. But deeper still, their presence is a symbol for many that the country is experiencing a period of peace. Time will tell if Buddhism, renowned as one of the world's most non-violent faiths, can eventually overturn the fact that, even today, disputes are often solved through conflict.

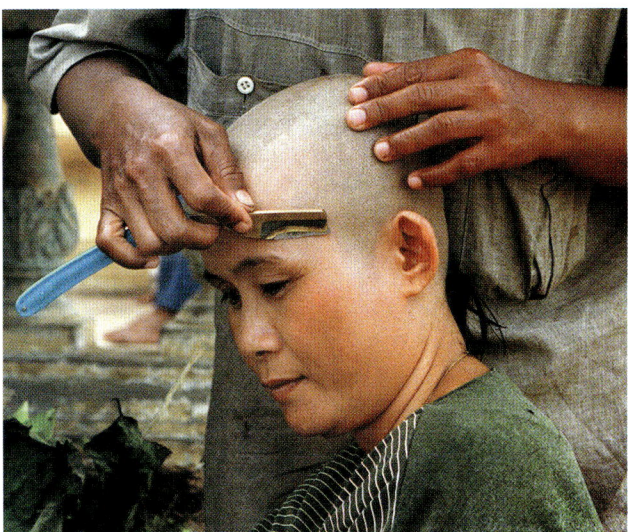

Above: A woman has her head shaved in preparation for becoming a nun.

Left: A monk finds something to smile about as he and his group shade themselves himself from the hot sun.

Above: Unable to afford to go to school, a girl instead sells flowers at a temple.

Left: A novice monk burns incense at a temple next to a large reclining Buddha.

Above: A child holds a bunch of flowers to sell to temple worshippers.

Right: An elderly monk keeps himself cool with a fan at an outdoor religious ceremony.

Novice monks return from collecting offerings at a nearby village.

A monk and his accessories add a splash of color to otherwise drab and dreary surroundings.

Left: A young monk shoulders a load of firewood as part of his daily chores.

Far left: A boy waits for offerings behind a row of monks during a Buddhist ceremony.

Below: A monk doles out medicine to a group of temple novices.

Above: Monks display the relaxed form of Buddhism that Cambodia is known for.

Right: A nun makes her donations as she moves along a row of monks.

Above: Monks find a block of cement in the Tonle Sap the ideal venue for a chat.

Right: Some monks do their best to keep their feet dry as they board a river ferry.

Monks on their way to a ceremony take an orderly shortcut through a cornfield.

PEOPLE

Above: A brother and sister sleep comfortably side by side in a makeshift hammock strung up at a pagoda.

Left: A girl carries her little sister with great care — children looking after children is a common sight throughout Cambodia.

The mathematics tell the story: according to the most conservative estimates, at least one million people — or one in seven of Cambodia's 1975 population — died under the Khmer Rouge. Since then the population has nearly doubled, with a large chunk of today's population under the age of twenty.

About ninety percent are ethnic Khmer (or Cambodian), but there is also a strong urban Chinese community, who make their presence felt in business and trade. There is a sizeable Vietnamese community — very much the underdog and often the hapless target of Cambodia's deep-felt frustrations with its bigger neighbor. Making a comeback are ethnic Cham — Muslims steadily finding their place in the diverse world of Islam and confidently reasserting their faith, after being virtually obliterated under the Khmer Rouge. In the distant north, and virtually off the map for many of their fellow countrymen, are a variety of isolated hill-tribe communities.

But what most people have in common is that they are desperately poor. Numerous countries have helped finance a new but basic infrastructure, but there is still no formal safety net in place to stop the underprivileged slipping further into misery. With corruption still running rife, the rich seem to get richer and the poor stay poor.

A child squats beside a tree as he sniffs glue — the cheap "high" is a major problem with street children in Phnom Penh.

A girl reveals where she hides the gemstones she found in a riverbed in the northern town of Pailin.

In a country where the past has been anything but calm, a woman sleeps peacefully.

Above: Hoping for handouts, peasants from the countryside travel to the city in the hope of some meager offerings.

Left: A monk comforts an orphaned child suffering from AIDS.

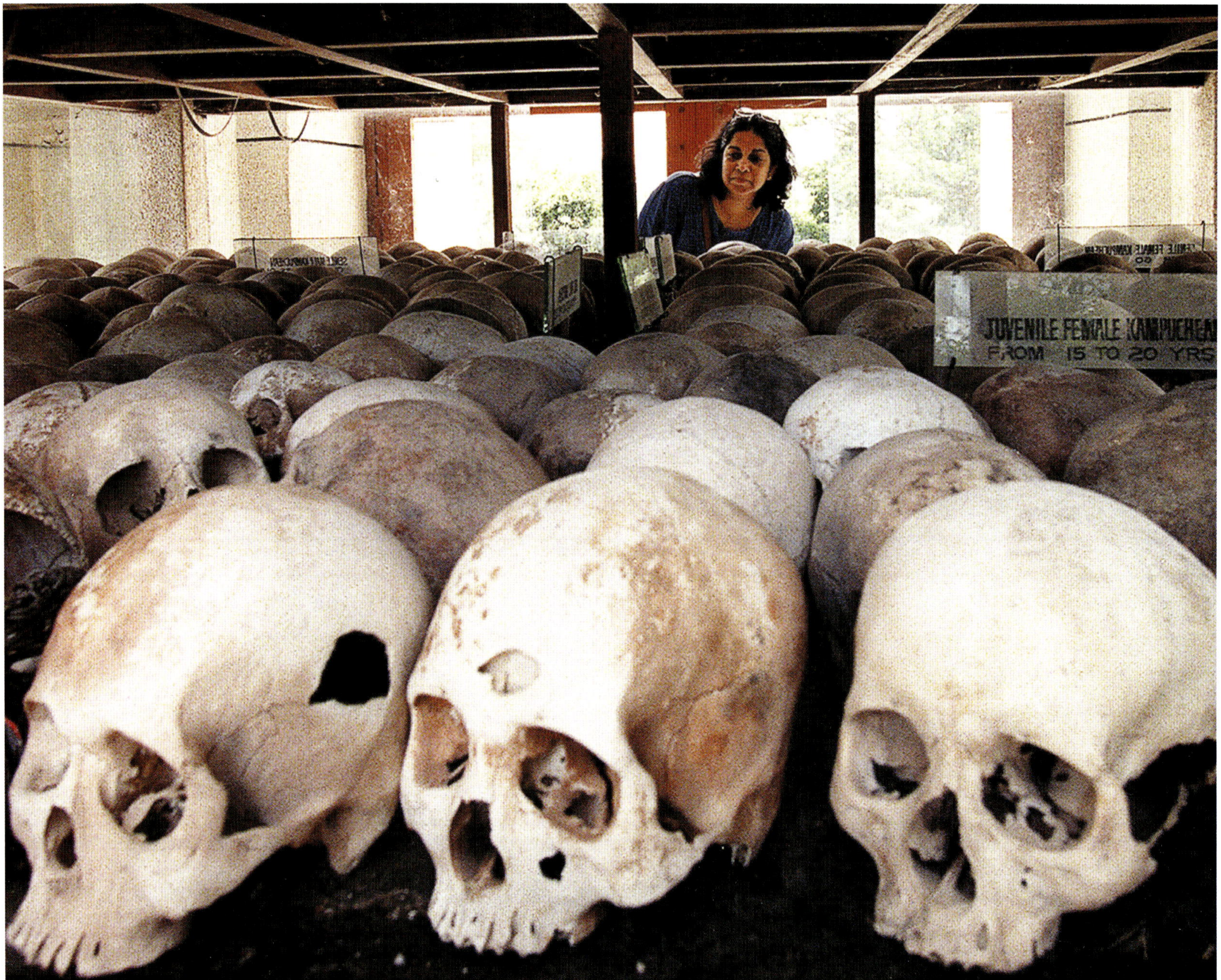
JUVENILE FEMALE KAMPUCHEAN
FROM 15 TO 20 YRS

Above: Remnants of the Khmer Rouge's genocidal brutality are there for all to see at the former S21 prison.
Left: A stark reminder of Cambodia's grim past, viewing skulls at the "Killing Fields" south of Phnom Penh.

A former soldier and land mine casualty watches two children play on the banks of the Tonle Sap.

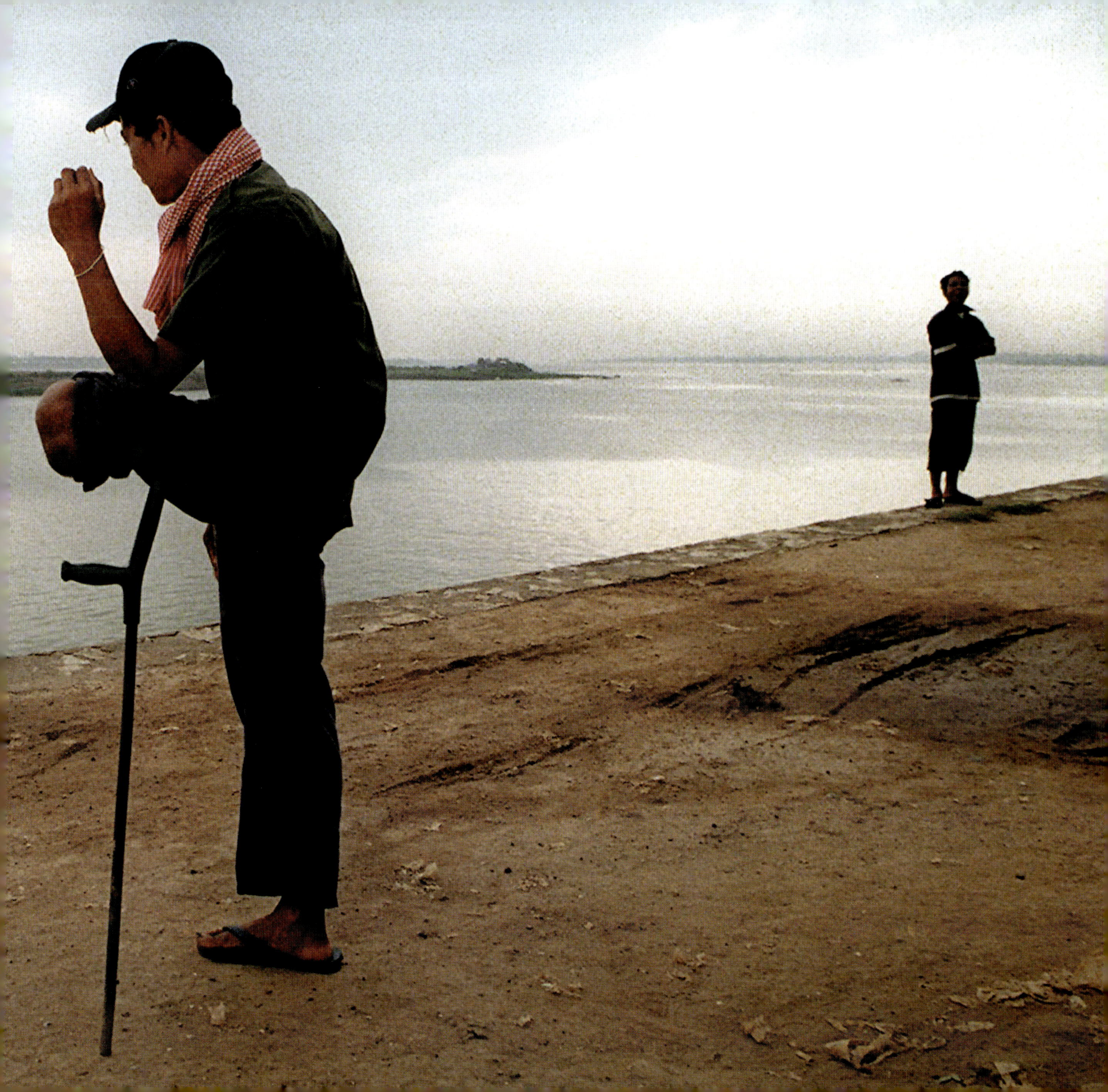

Top: A cyclo driver signals to traffic as he carries a mother and her inquisitive child.

Above: Riding together in tandem, cyclos transport a group of women to a ceremony.

Children enlist the help of a cyclo to get their goods to an early morning market.

A child barely has room to fit as a cyclo carries a hefty load of boxes.

Following pages: Proudly carrying their lengthy conquest, a group of children lug a python home.

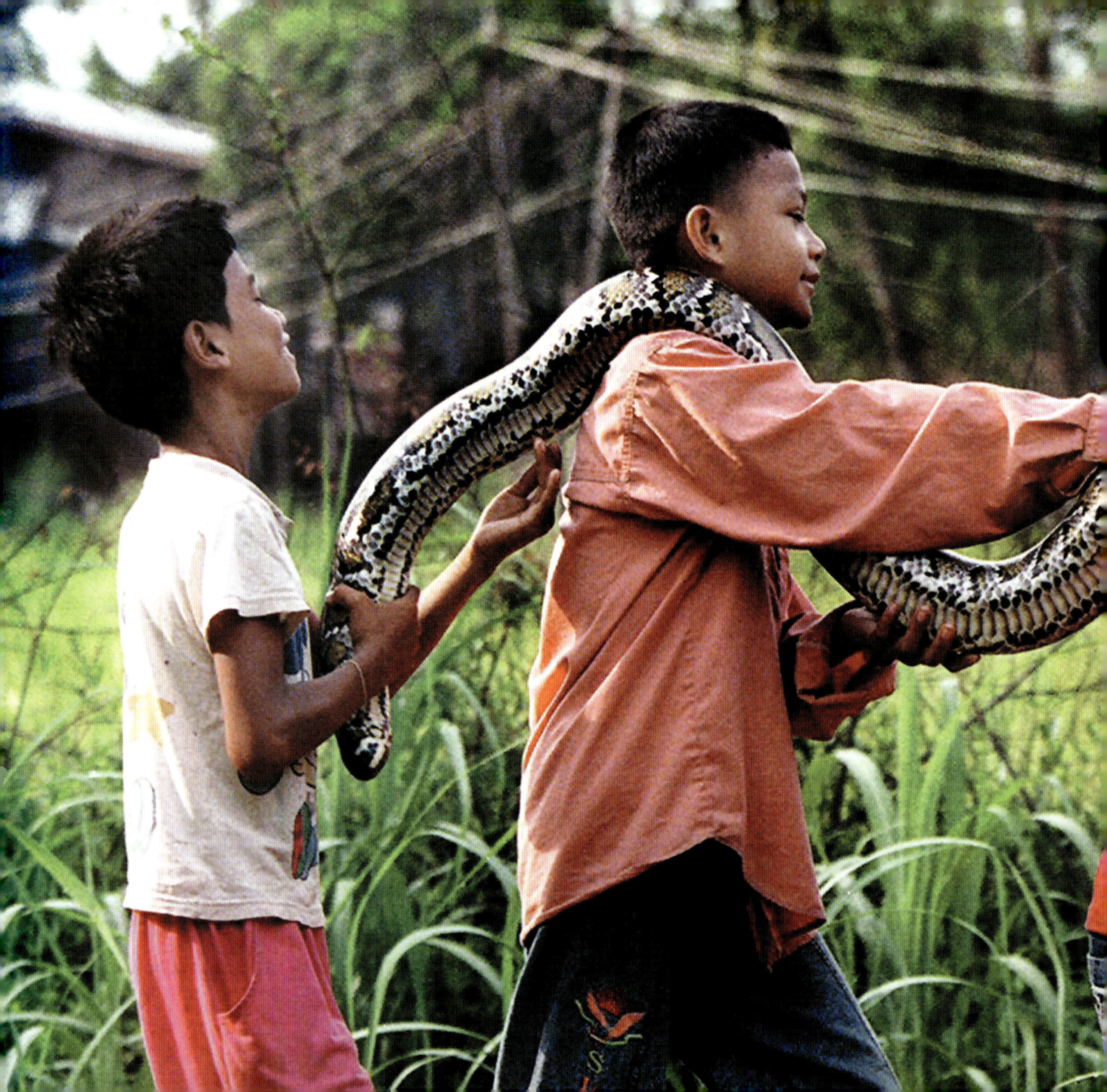

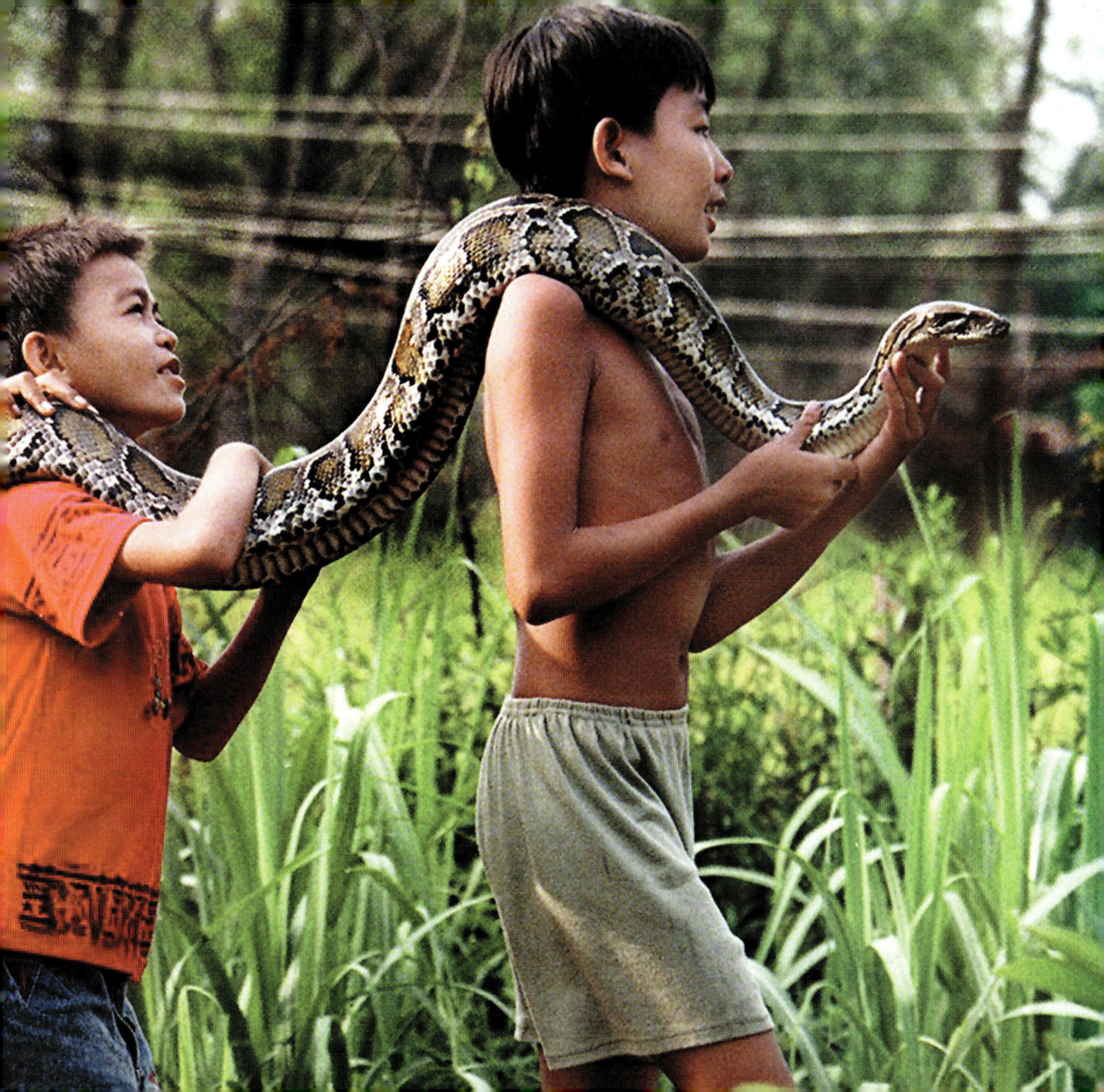

A cyclo driver braves the floods as he ferries his passenger through the back streets.

A motto rider plows through rising floodwaters in Phnom Penh as workers remove a large portrait of Queen Monineath.

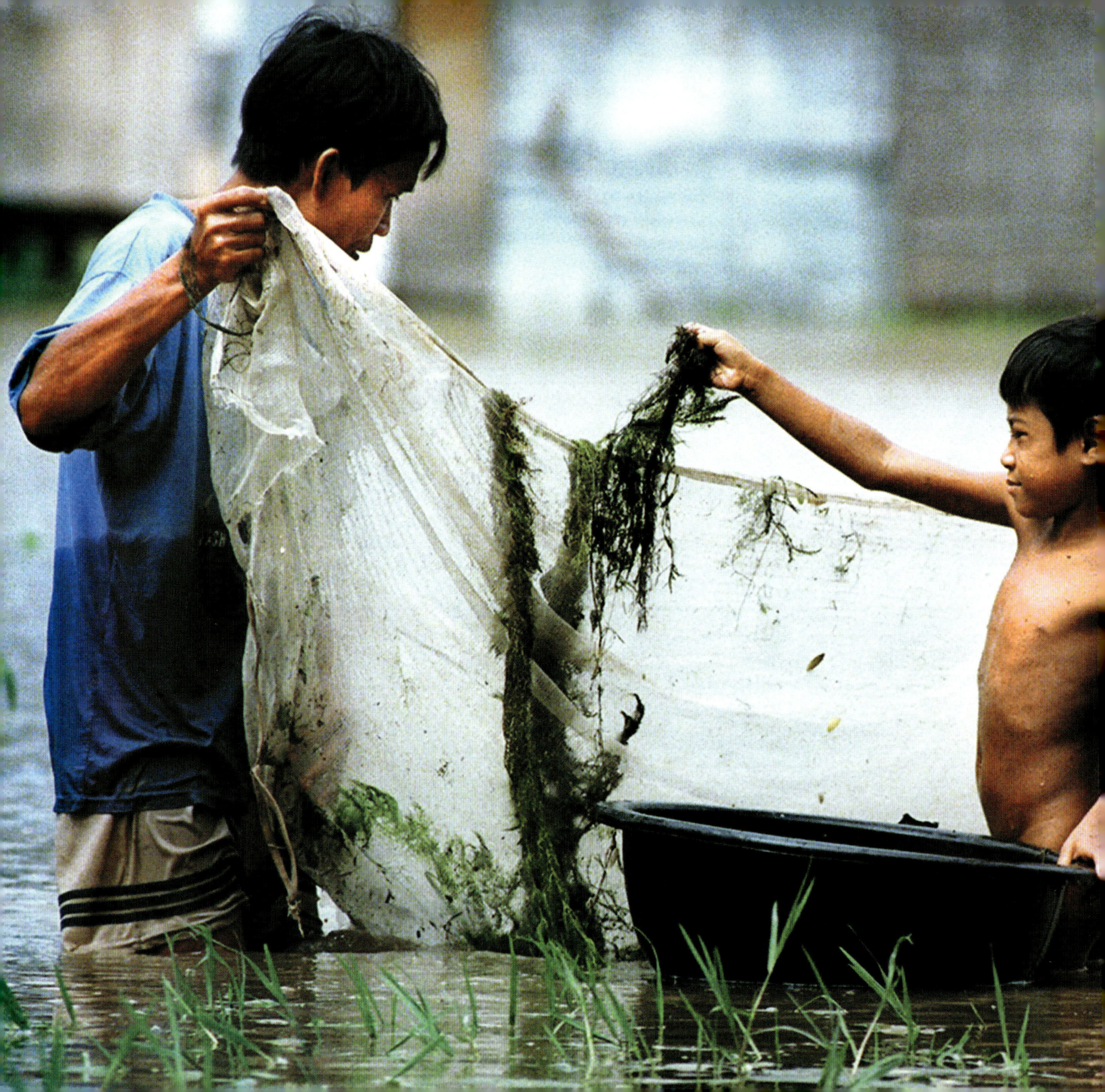

Above: Villagers head for higher ground as floods submerge their homes.

Left: A family tries their luck in the floodwaters, hoping to catch small fish to add to their meal.

Taking full advantage of wash day, children play in the water near a jetty.

Washing, bathing, or fishing — Cambodians share the Tonle Sap for various activities.

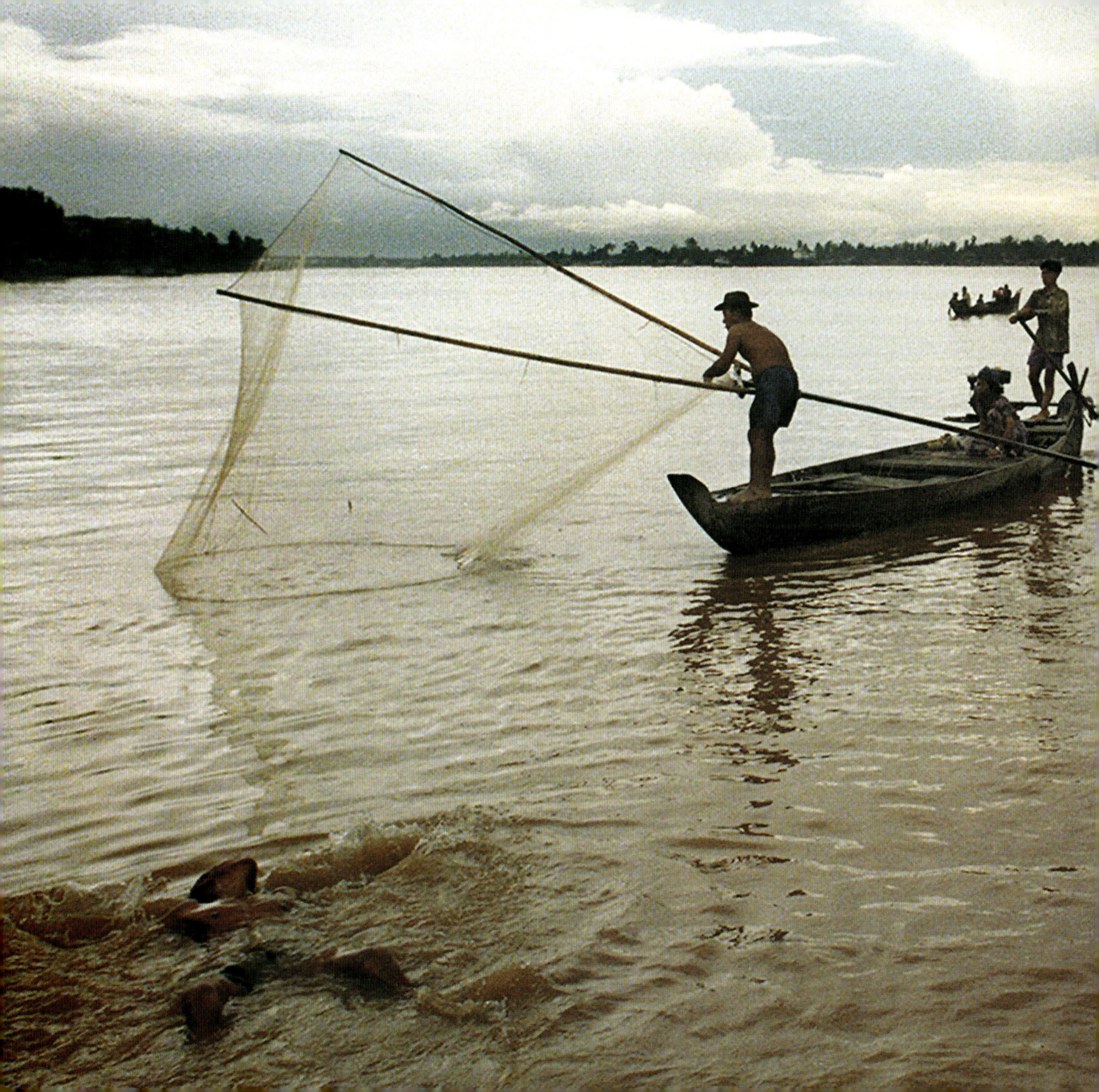

Above: Silhouetted against glistening waters, a fisherman casts his Y-framed scoop net.

Left: A child plays as a fisherman ekes out a living from the Tonle Sap.

53

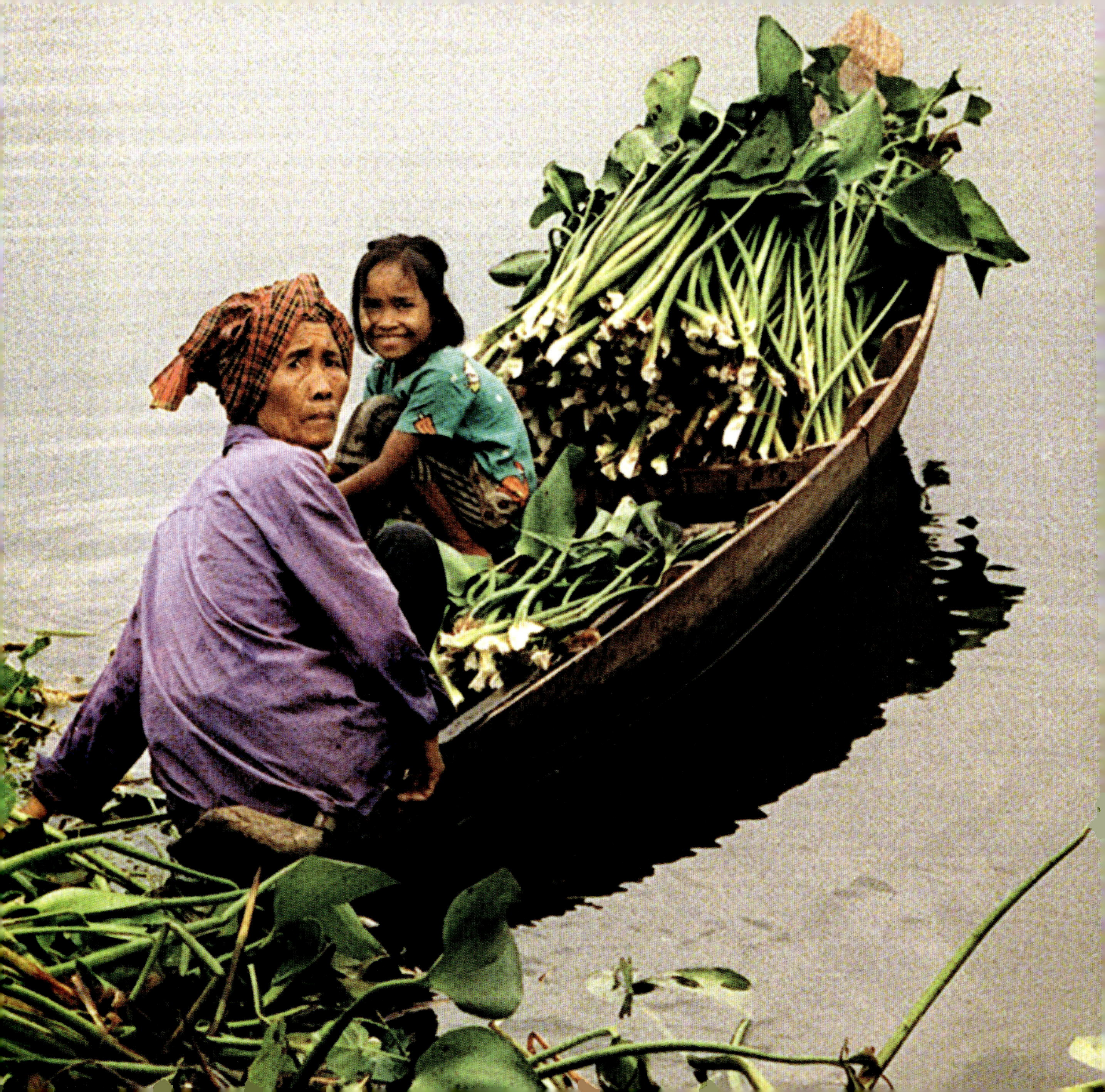

Left: A customer makes a selection from a vegetable stall manned by children.

Far left: A woman and child pile their boat up high with water plants.

Below Left: Straight from a boat, a woman heads for market with a basket full of fresh water plants and vegetables.

Below: Who needs a wheelbarrow when your head will do?

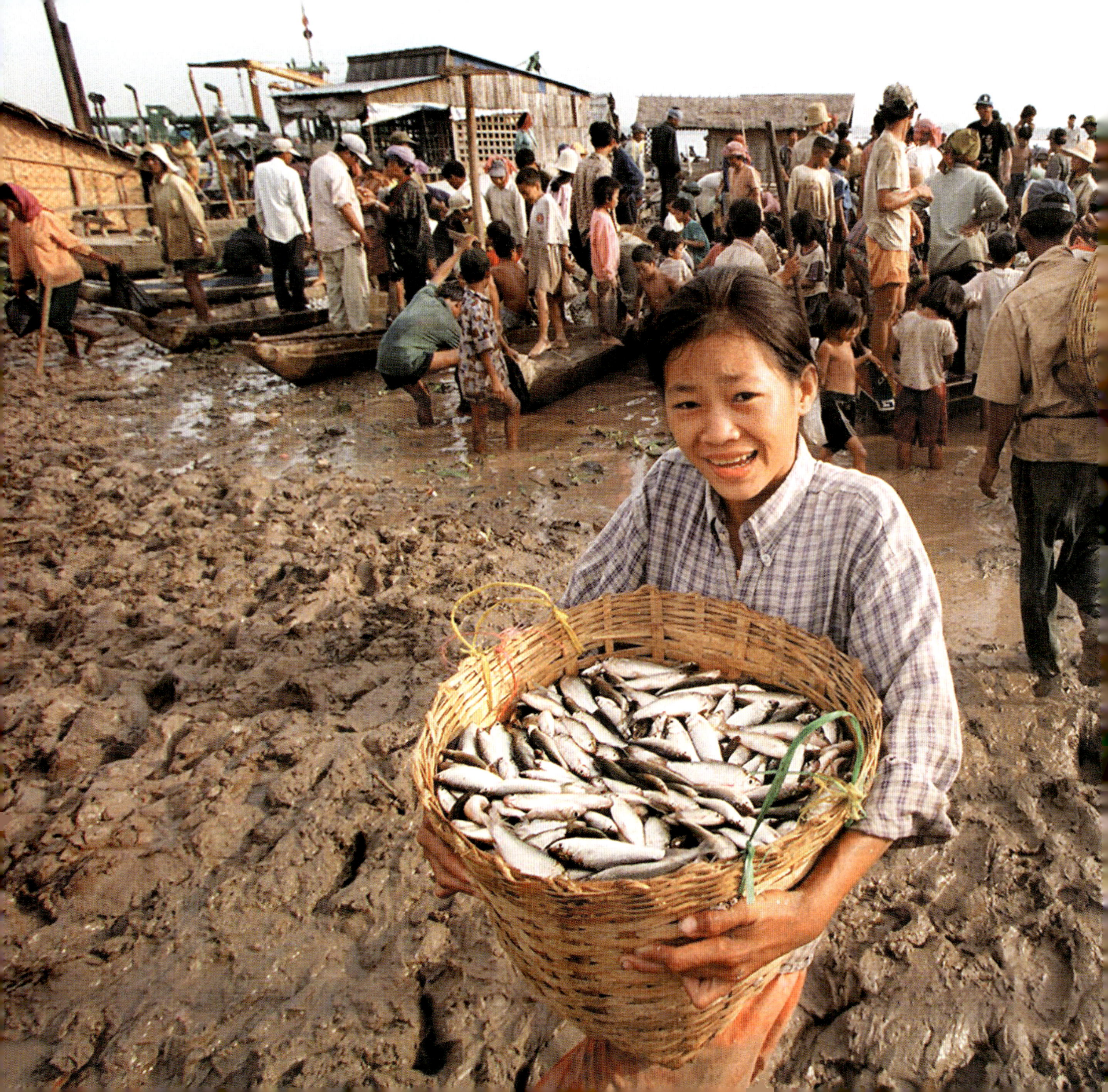

Above: A man enthusiastically uses his feet to mash small fish for fermenting later into a Cambodian delicacy.

Left: A young girl makes her way off the muddy banks of the Tonle Sap with a basket of freshly caught fish destined for the market.

Following pages: Passengers opt for the cheap seats on a train between Phnom Penh and Sihanoukville.

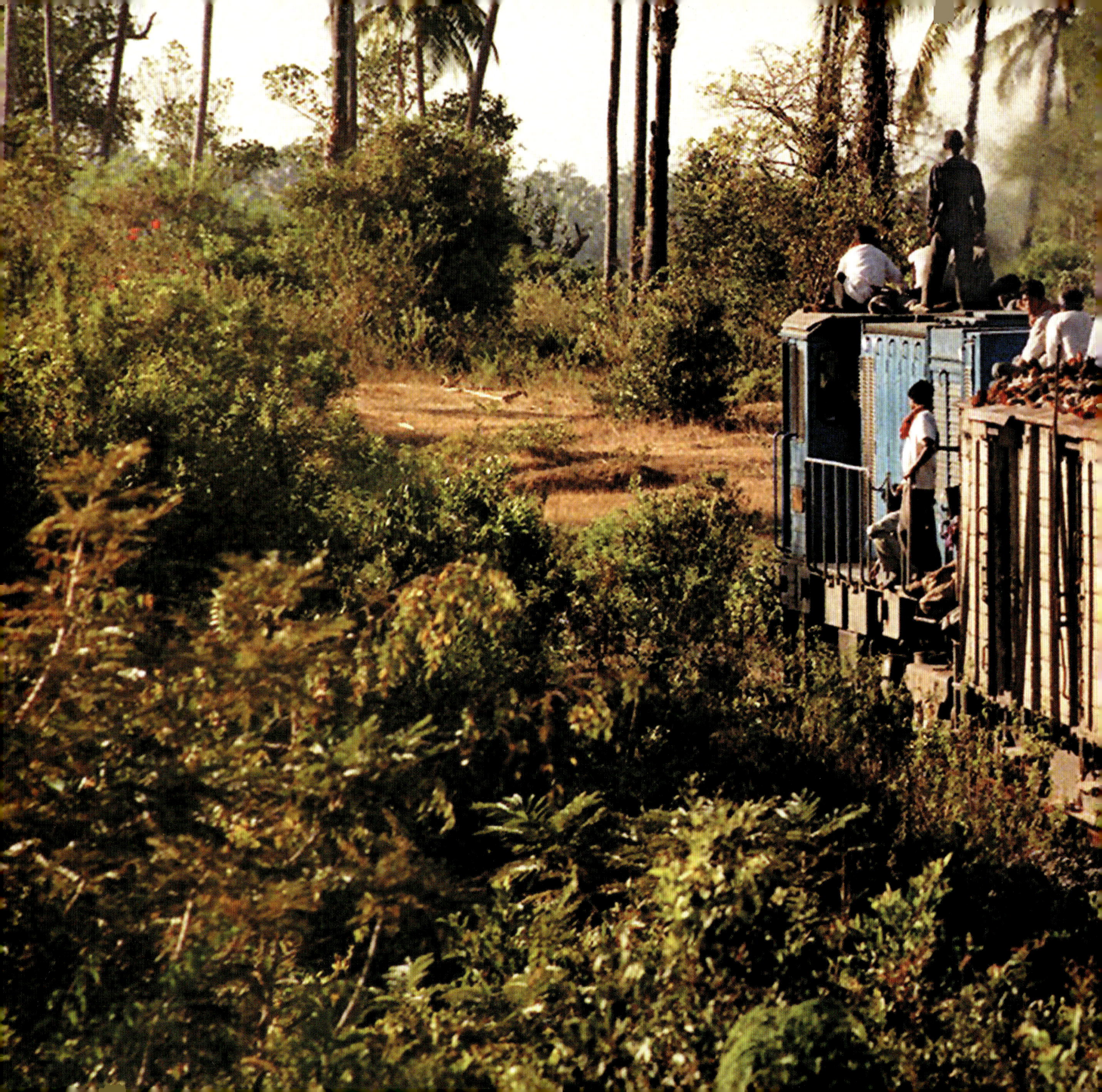

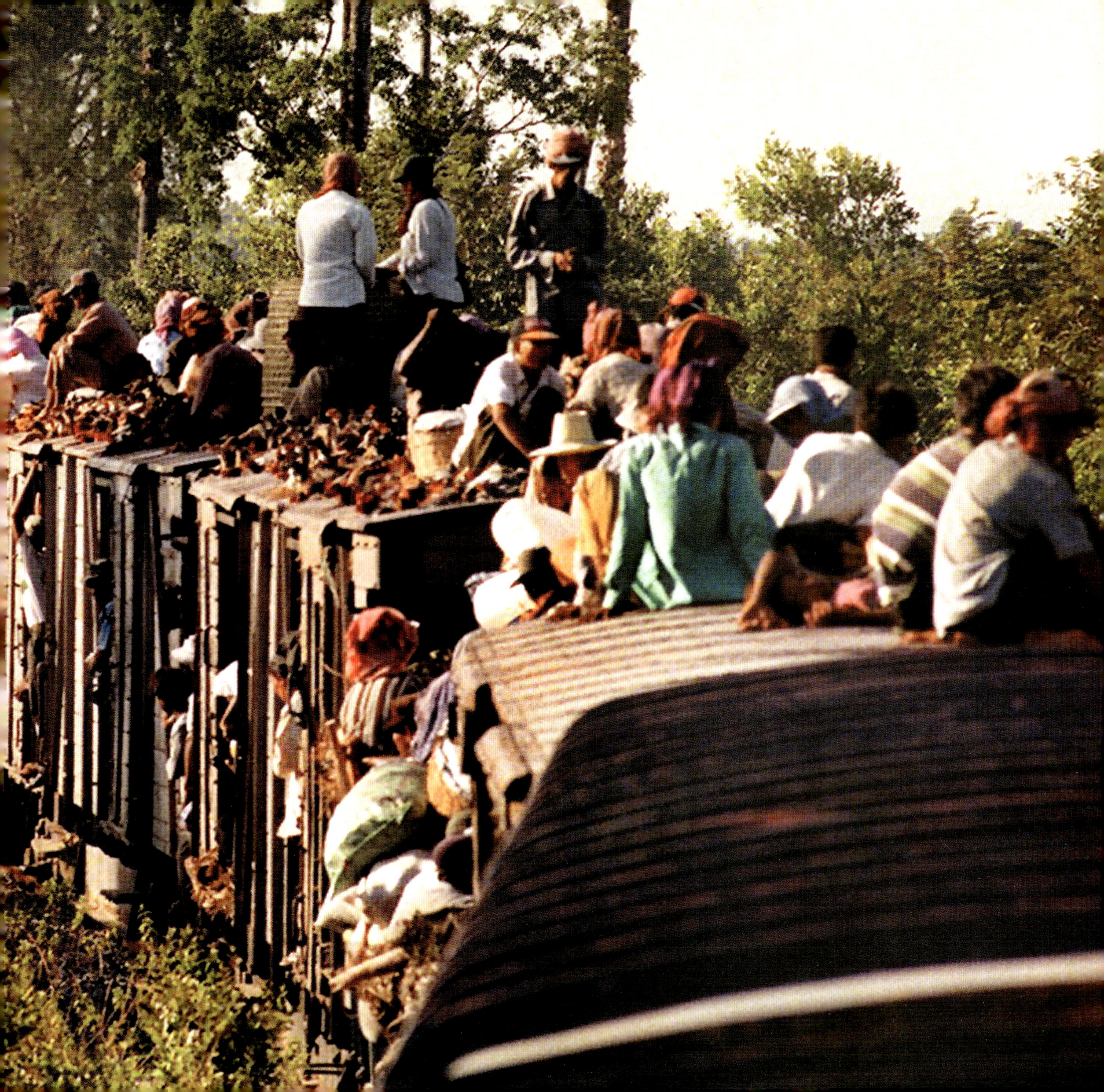

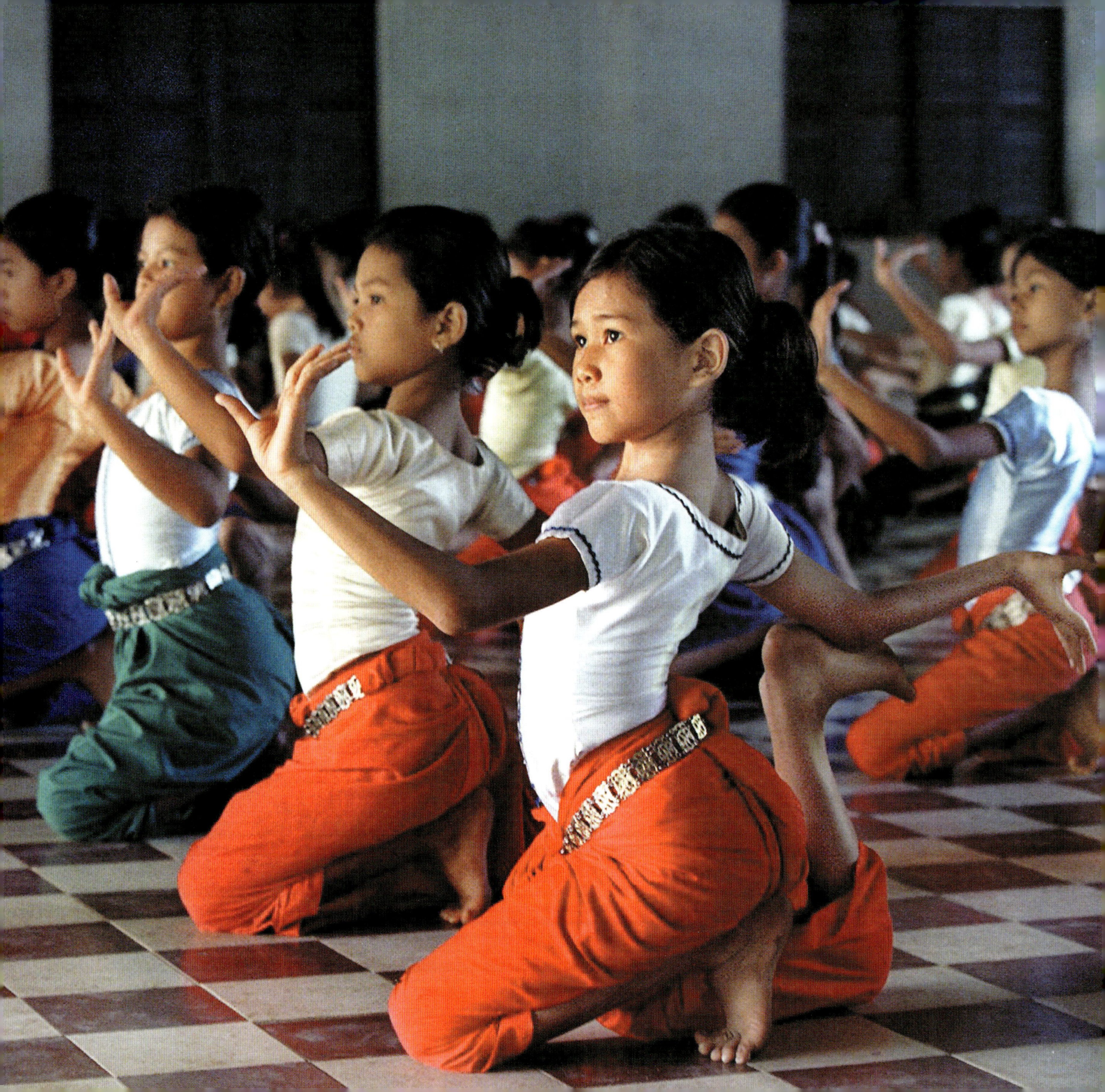

CULTURE

Cambodia's culture is in a phase of both revival and unprecedented change. On the one hand are the survivors of decades of war, who are once again rediscovering their roots and customs, such as dance, drama, and music that have been unchanged for centuries. Then there is the younger generation, increasingly looking to the outside world and providing a social transformation. Marriages are now less class-driven or pre-arranged affairs, access to schooling has jumped, and nightclubs have sprung up, while increased safety on the highways — a very recent phenomenon — has led to unprecedented social mobility. Increased trade has also has a major impact: traditional music is being challenged by Thai-style pop, while the markets are packed with pirated Hollywood movies, which find their way into the country almost overnight, thanks to well-connected networks of relatives in the United States.

Another transformation is in the workplace: unions are beginning to raise their voice against any investors who think Cambodia's pool of cheap labor can be easily exploited. Labor laws are steadily being enforced, providing people — for the first time — with leisure time.

Above: A young performer awaits a cue for her next performance.

Left: Cambodian children practice the graceful techniques of Khmer dancing.

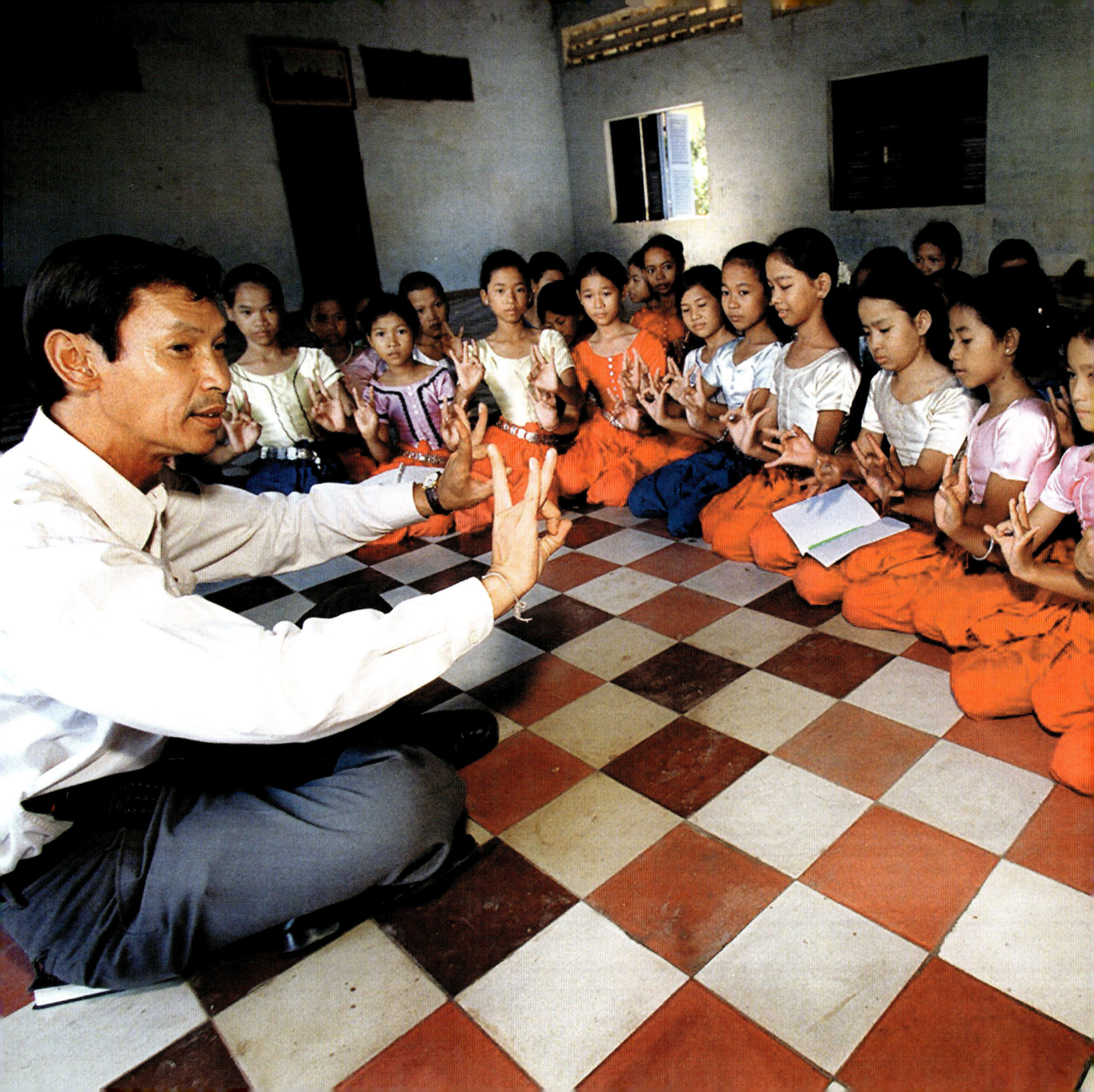

Left: A young Apsara dancer in traditional dress concentrates intently as she practices.

Far Left: A teacher instructs children in the finer techniques of using hands in Khmer dancing.

Below: Apsara dancers perform at an official ceremony — each girl trains for years to perfect her demanding art.

63

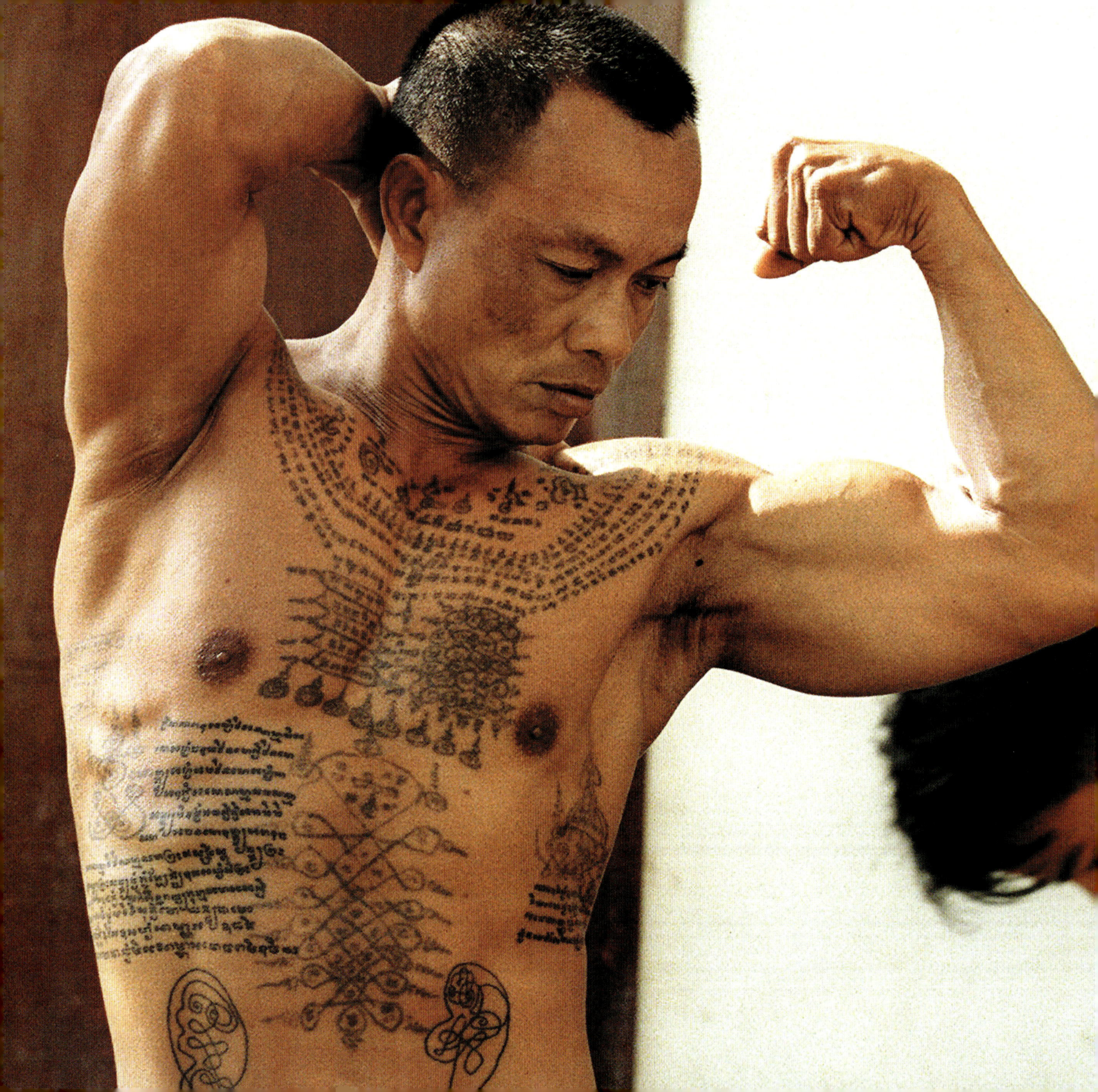

Above: Participants in Cambodia's first ever bodybuilding competition strike their poses.

Left: A bodybuilding competitor flexes his muscles, and his tattoos, before he takes to the stage.

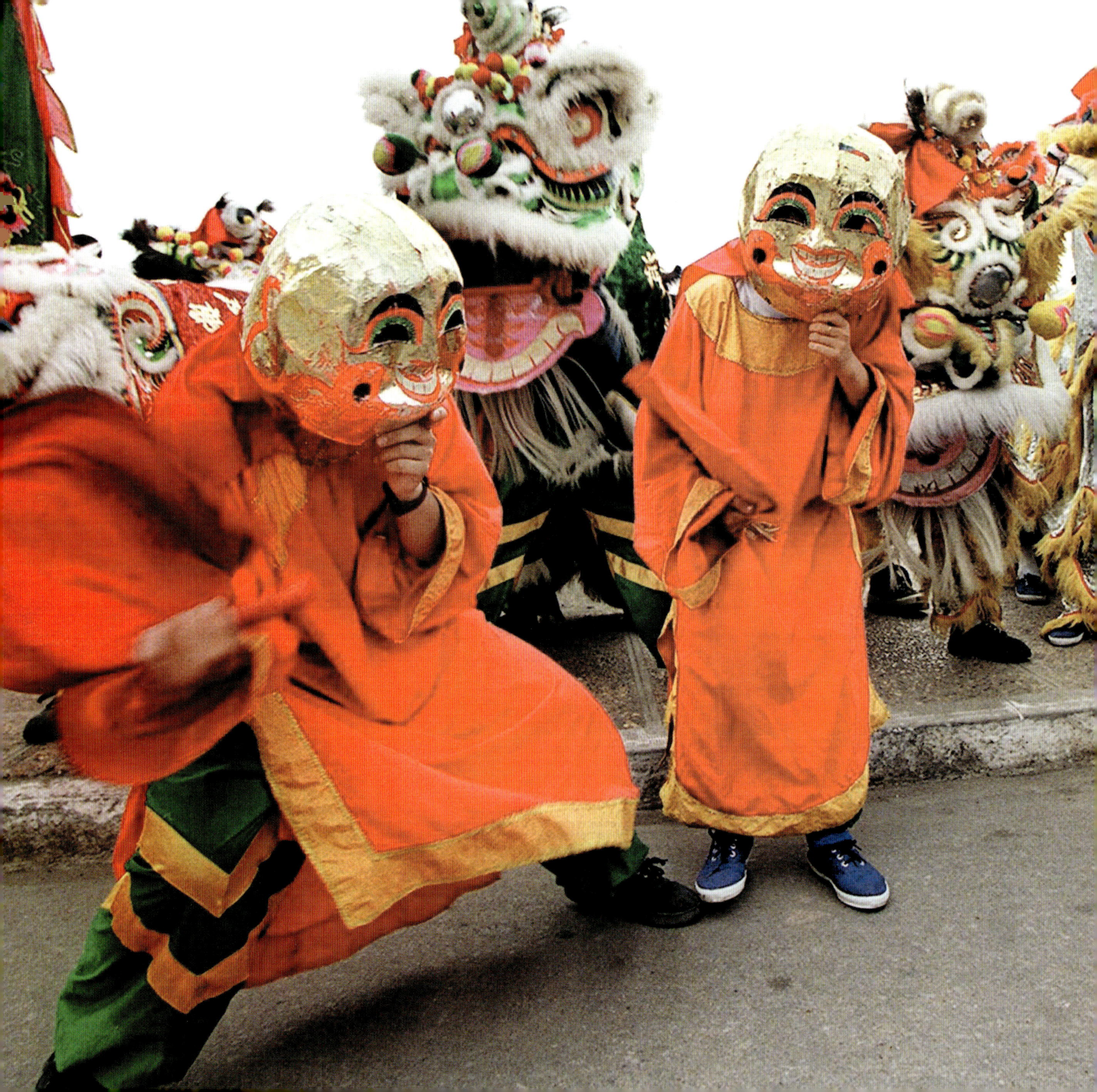

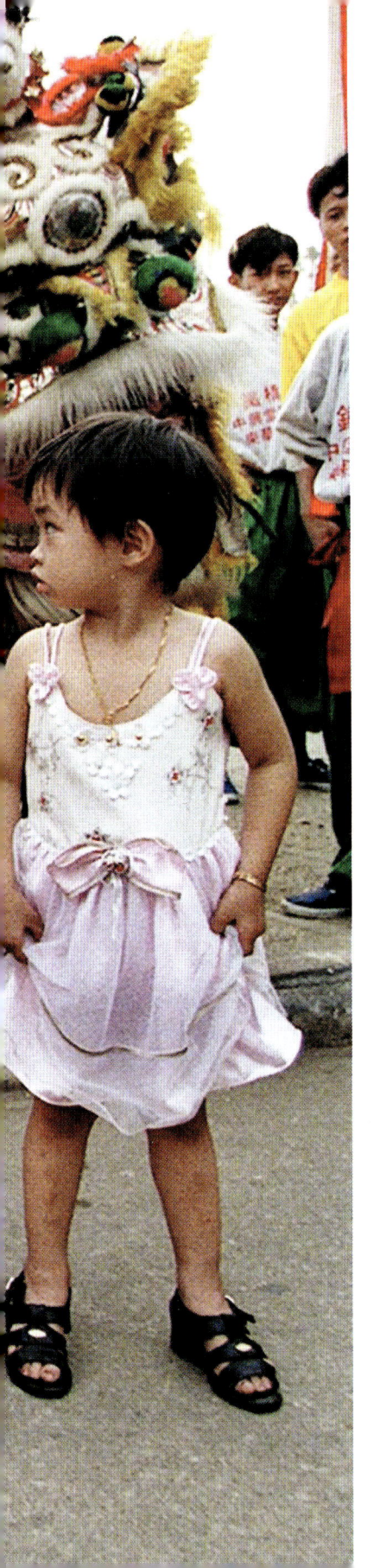

Above: Proudly holding a discarded Santa doll, a young girl beams at finding her garbage dump treasure.

Left: Half intrigued and half apprehensive, a little girl watches dragon dancers celebrating the arrival of the Chinese New Year.

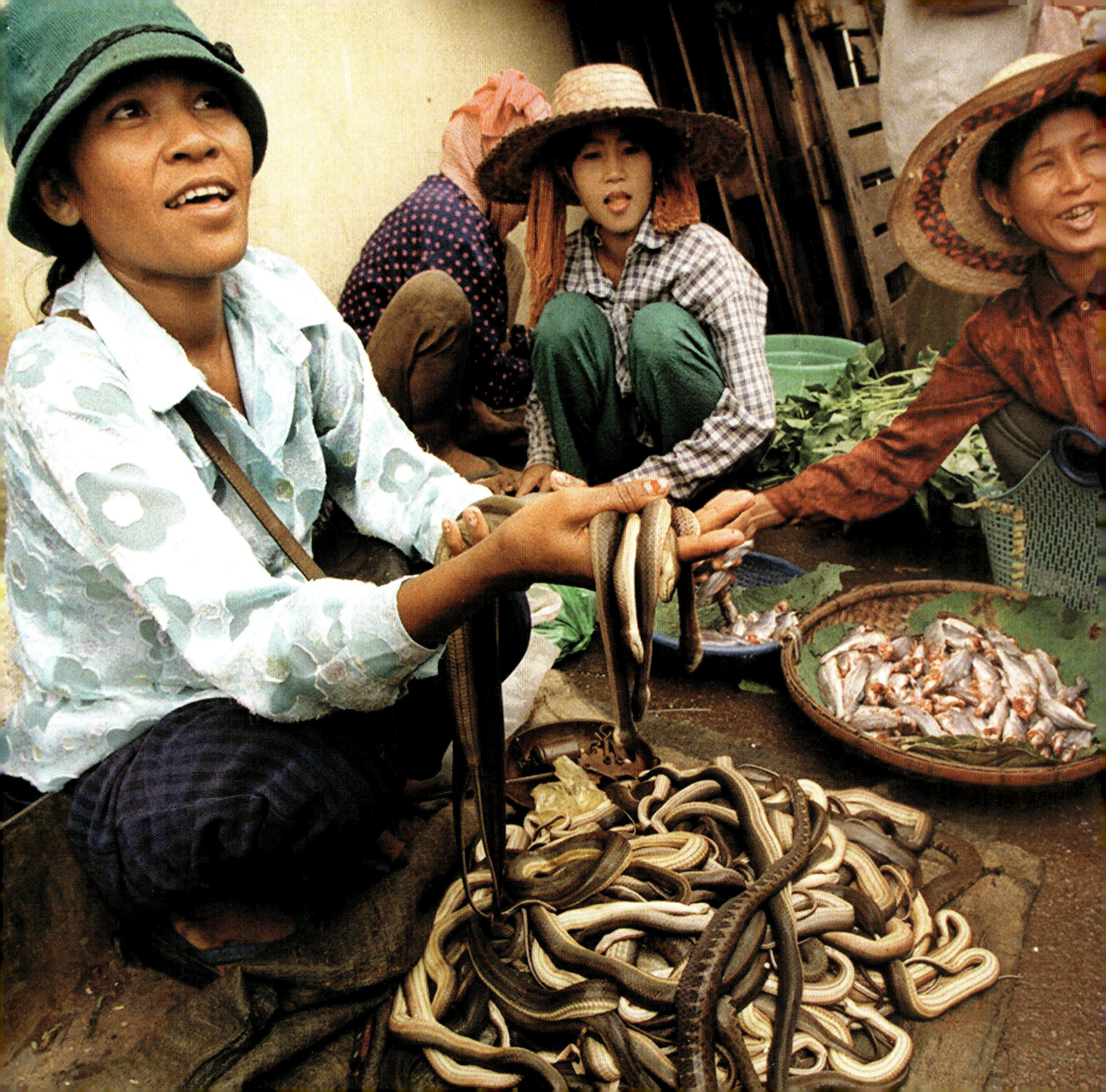

THE ECONOMY

Above: Helping feed a hungry population, rice seedlings are harvested.

Left: Women in a market produce their exotic assortment of snakes for sale.

Fish, rice, and foreign aid are the mainstays of the economy. Most Cambodians live a subsistent existence, surviving on a basic diet of fish, rice, and fruits regardless of whether they live in the cities or countryside. For most, daily life can only be described as a struggle: a struggle to make ends meet, battling the harsh landscape and relative lack of natural resources.

But there is timber: a controversial subject, because all factions in recent decades have sought to make a quick and easy buck at the expense of Cambodia's vast expanse of forest habitat. The industry today is subject to close monitoring, but the risk of widespread deforestation remains as neighboring countries look to exploit local corruption and porous borders, regardless of Cambodia's delicate ecosystem. The results are sometimes hard-felt in the monsoon season, when the country's lifeblood: the Tonle Sap lake and Mekong River approach bursting point.

A few also eke out a living through rubber production and gemstones, notably rubies. Mines are open cast pits of mud along former Khmer Rouge strongholds at the western border with Thailand. Blasts of high-powered water jets are followed by thousands of scavengers armed with wide pans. But visitors looking for cheap stones beware: local dealers also carry an array of fake, Western-produced copies that can fool the eye of anyone who is not an expert.

All in all, Cambodia's estimated twelve million-strong population scrapes together a GDP per head of under US$1000 dollars per year, ranking the country as one of the poorest in Asia, if not the world.

Vital support comes from foreign aid, distributed by legions of expatriate staff that come and go, as national governments compete for their piece of influence.

Above: A farmer urges a pair of water buffalo to work harder.

Right: Man and beast combine together as part of the rice production process.

Following pages: Women, ankle-deep in water, plant rice seedlings in a rice paddy just outside the capital.

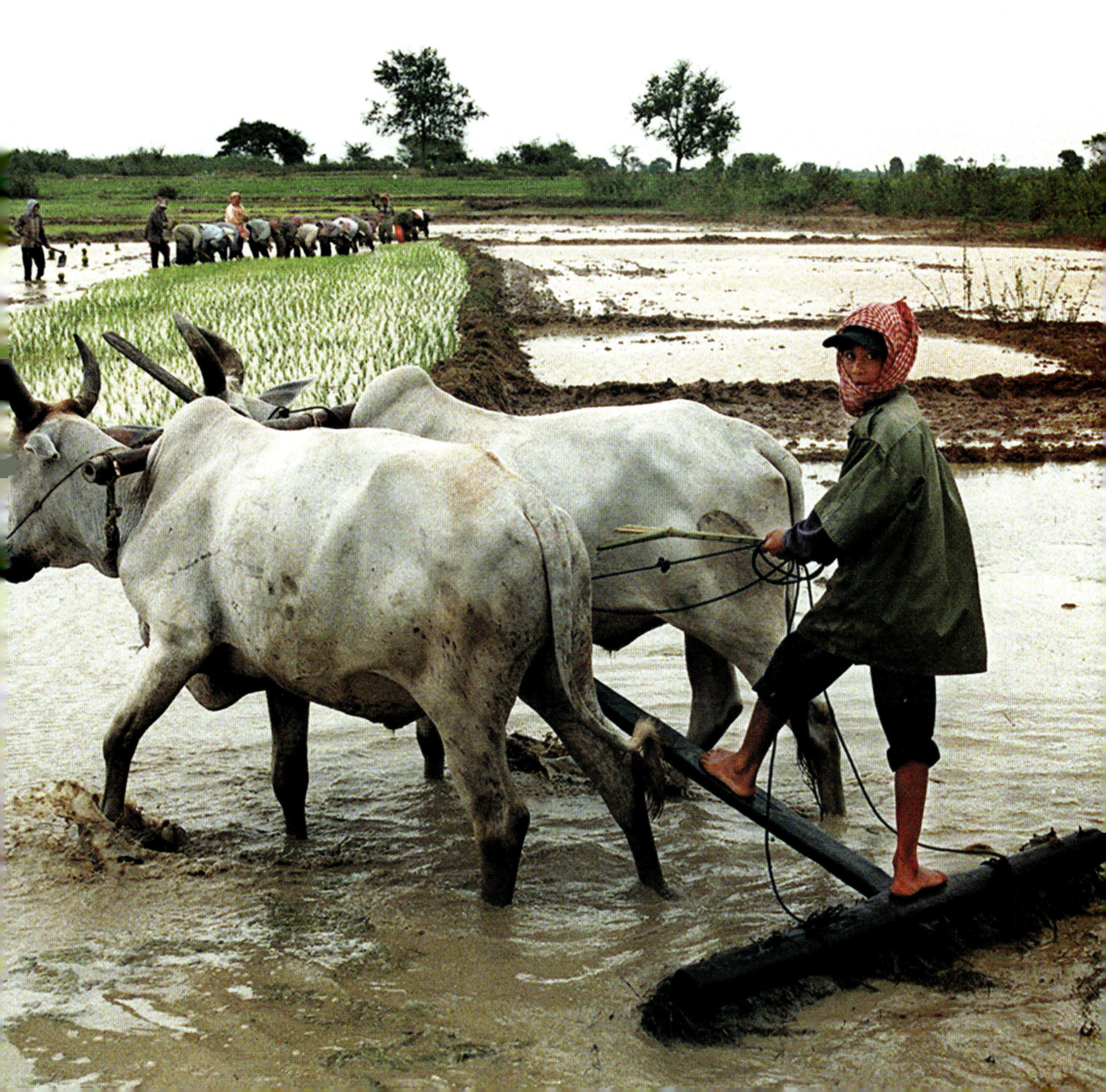

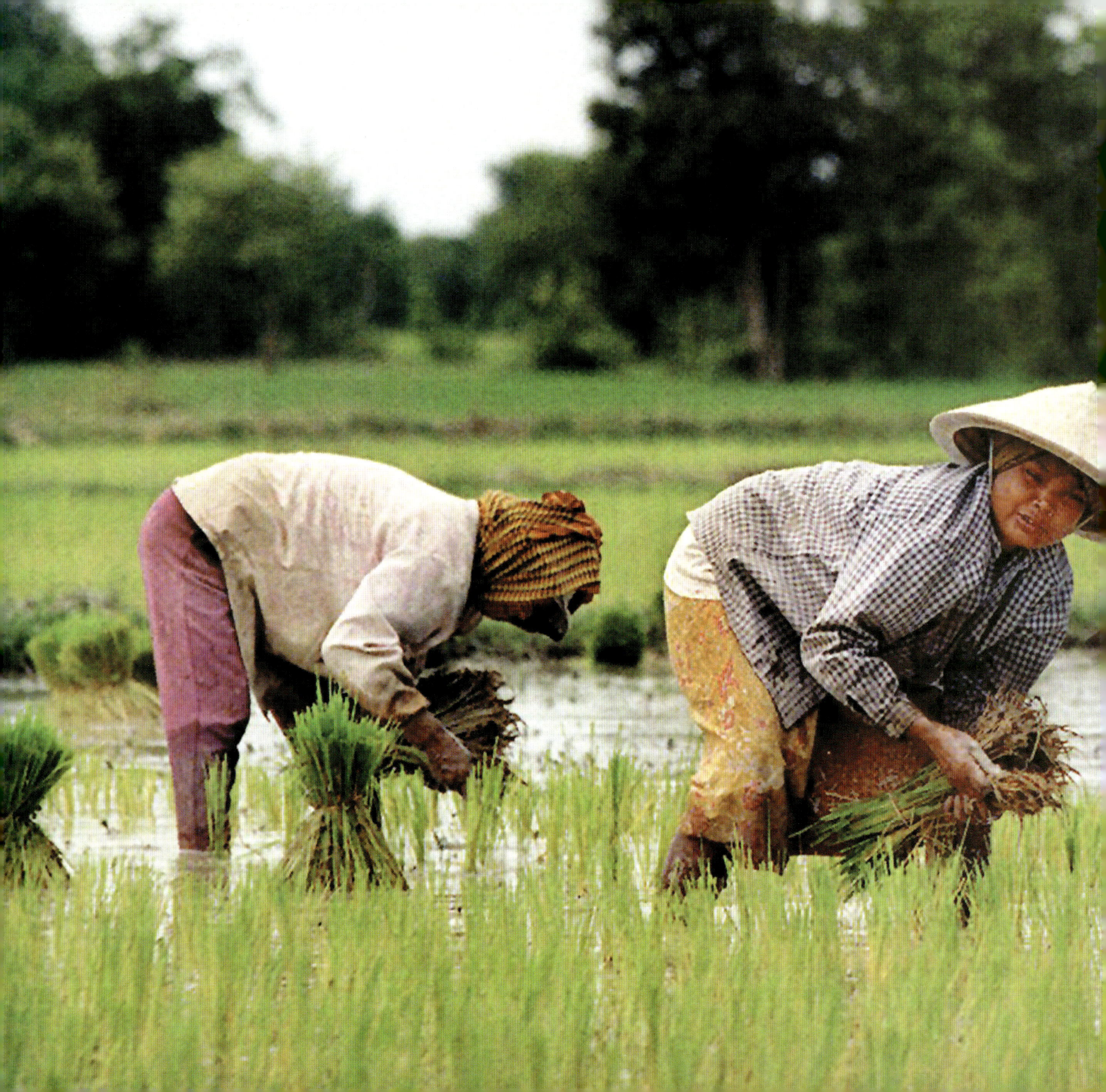

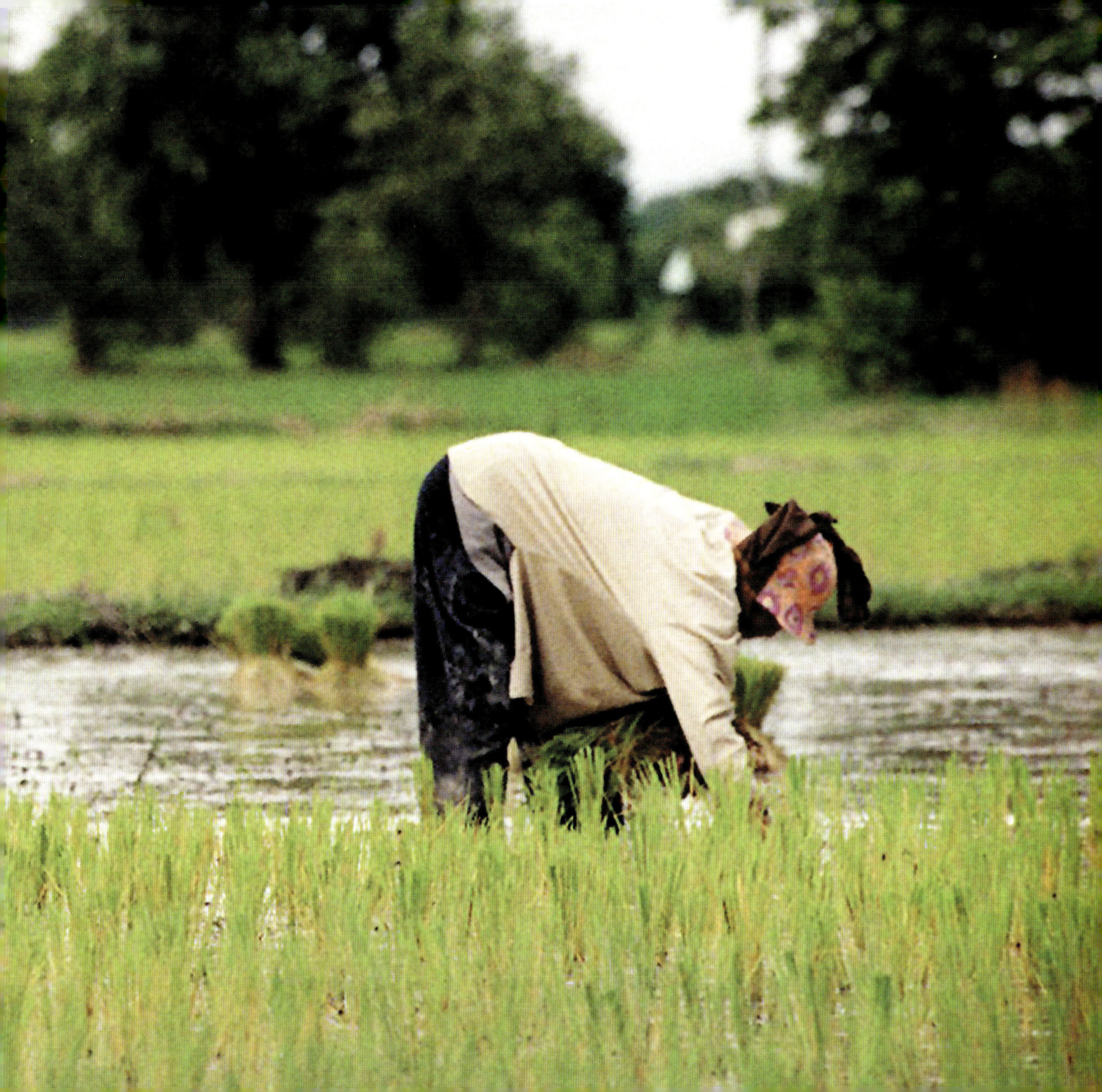

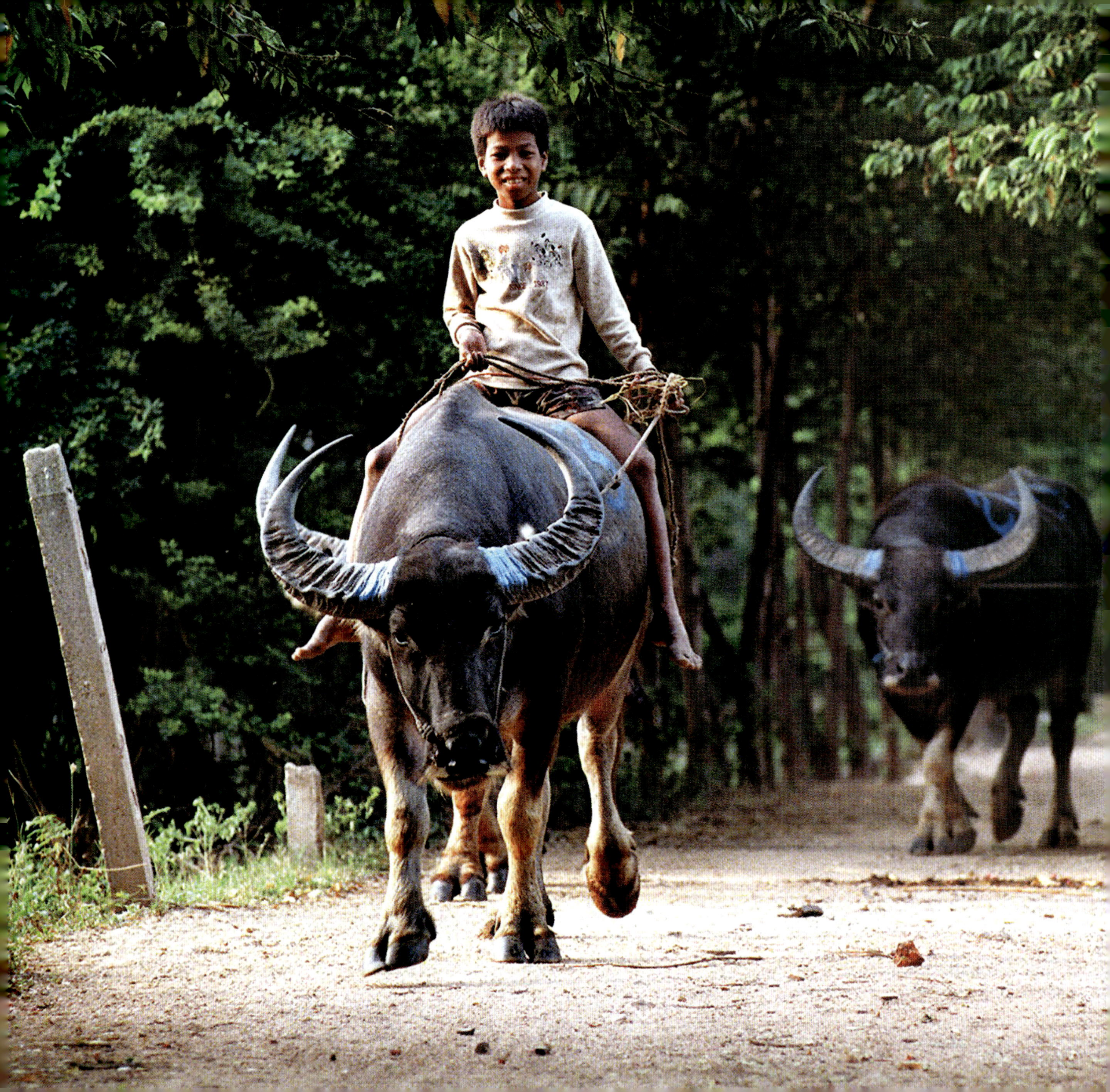

Above: When not ploughing paddies, buffaloes are often looked after by small boys.

Left: Heading for pastures anew, a boy opts to ride as his companion decides on a more sedate approach.

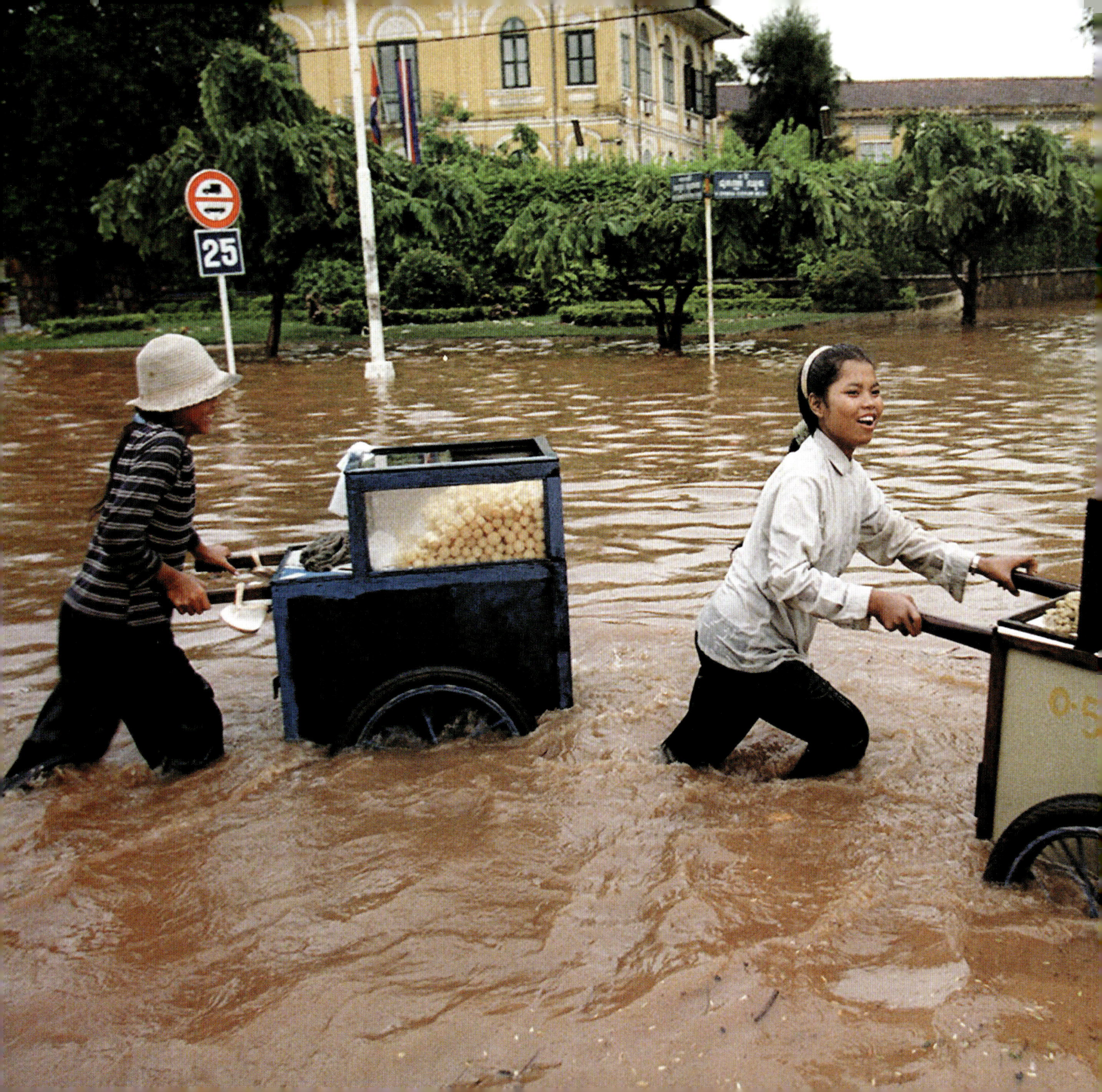
25

Top: A girl fans hot coals as she cooks corn cobs at a roadside stall.

Above: Two women push their mobile pillow and cushion shop through the streets.

Left: Caught out by floodwaters, two sugarcane sellers are still all smiles.

Above: Steam engulfs a cook preparing noodles at a market stall.

Right: A french stick seller catches a quick roadside breakfast.

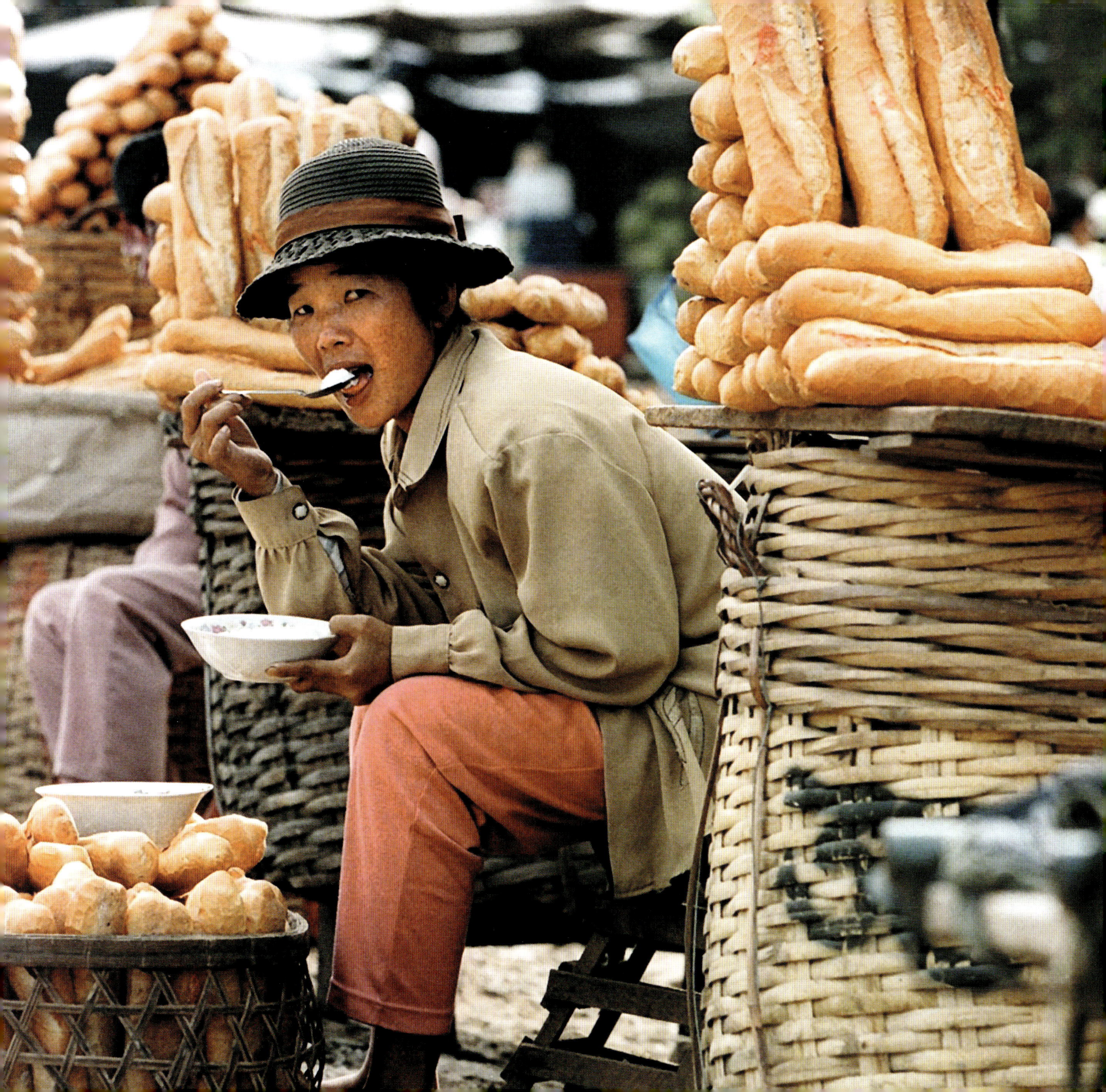

Cambodia's streets are a showcase for Cambodians' entrepreneurial flair.

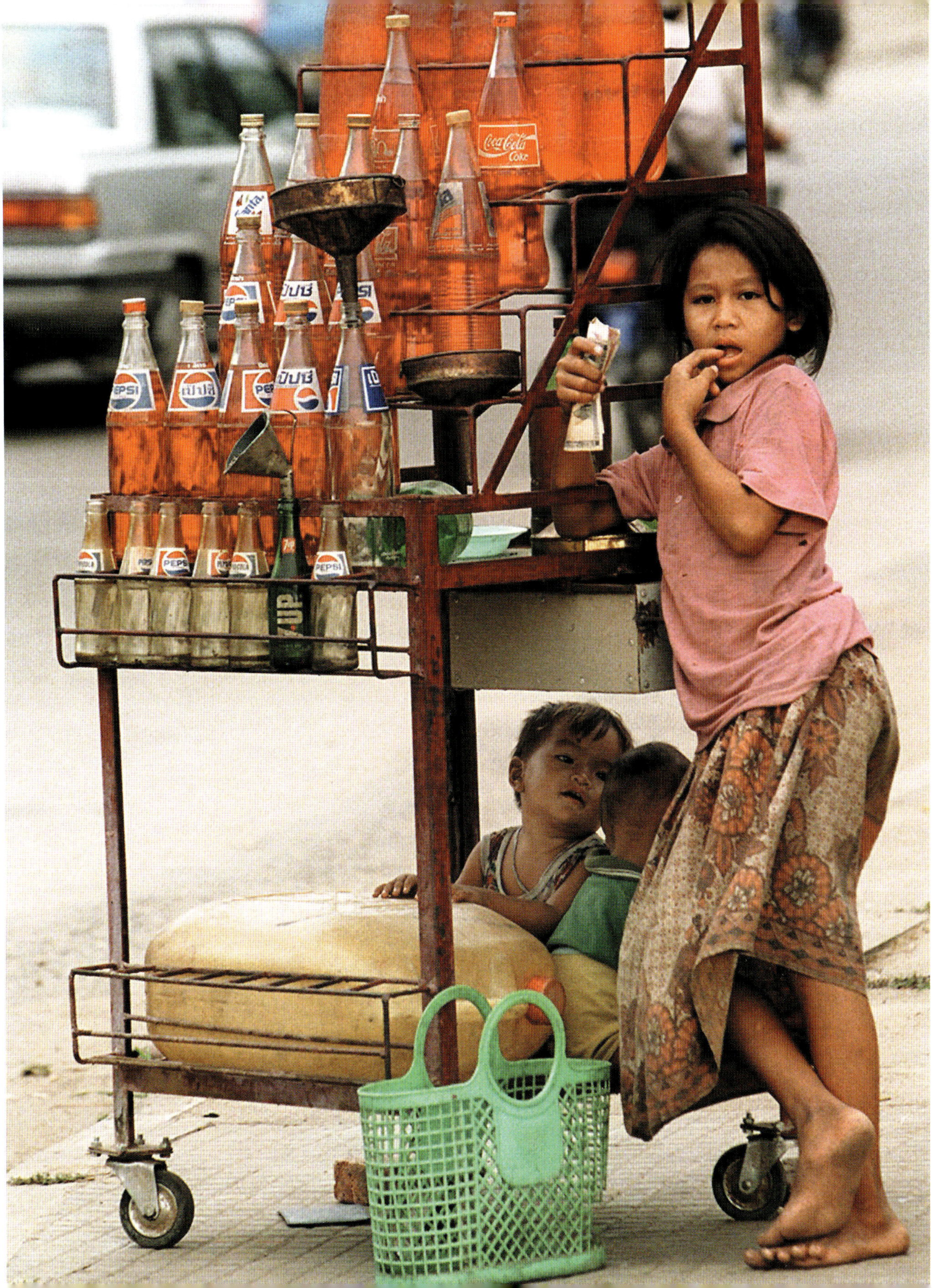
PEPSI
Coca-Cola
Coke

Scavenging at garbage dumps is the only way of making a living for some Cambodians.

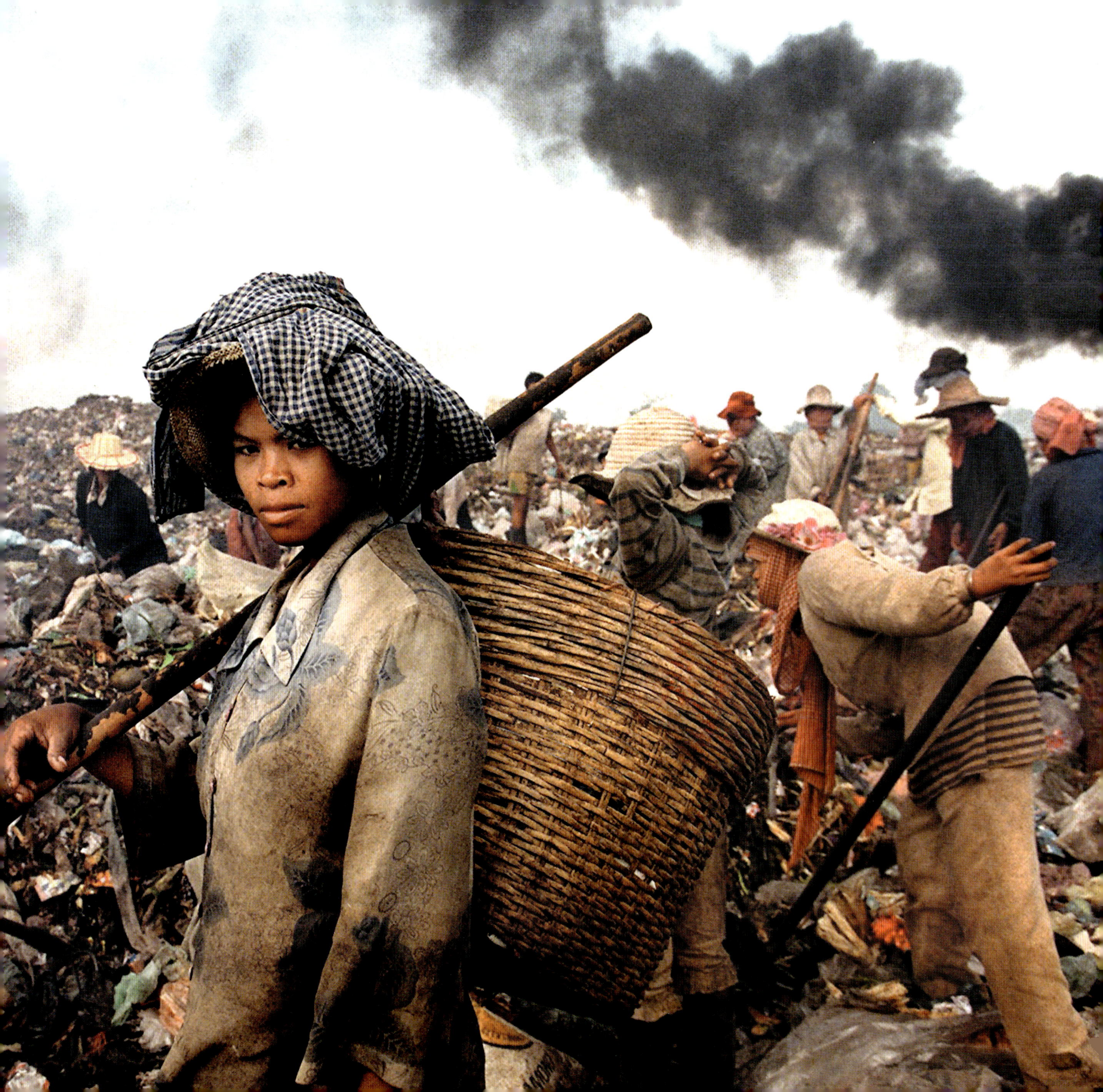

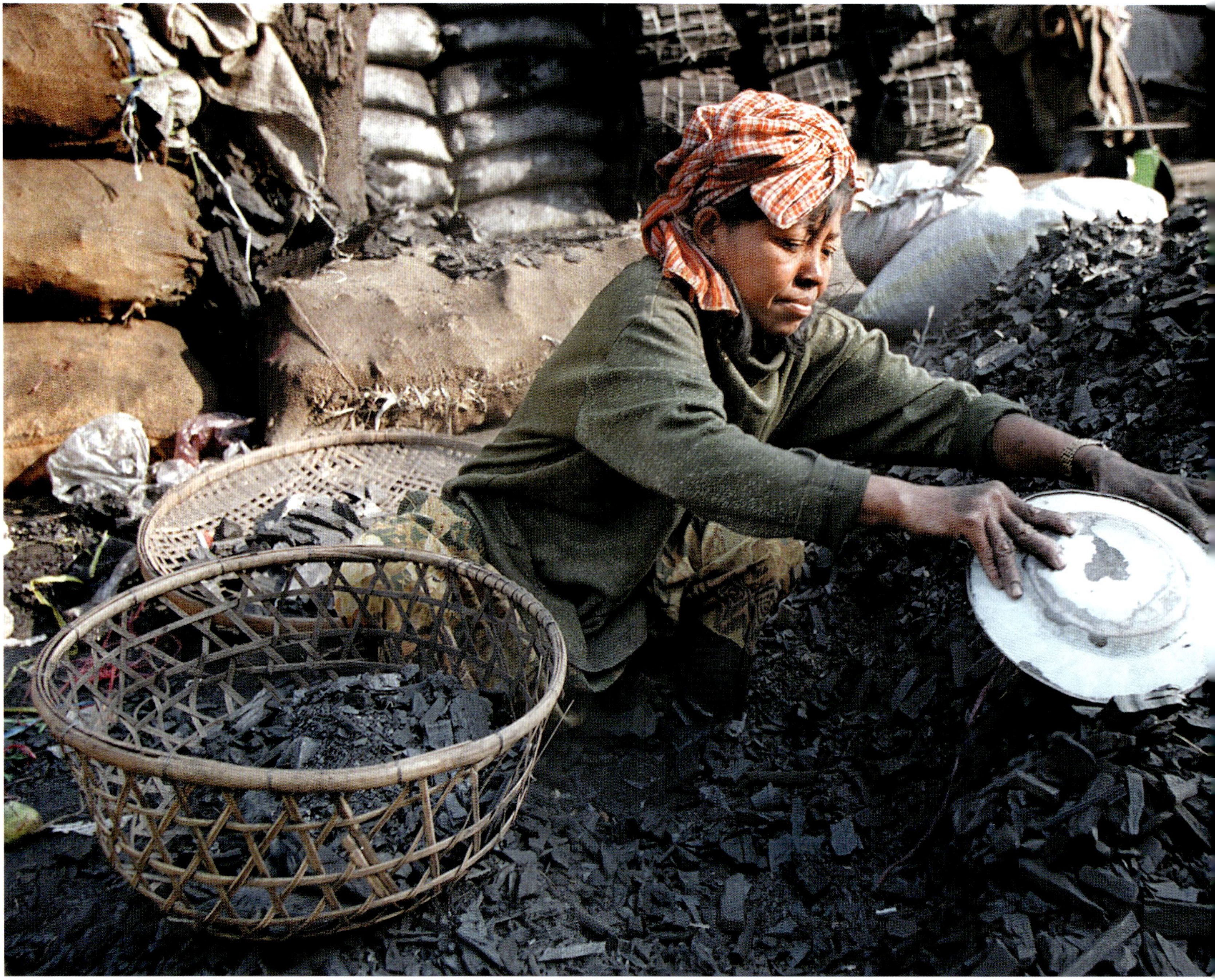

Left: Linemen make repairs among a hazardous maze of electrical wires.

Far left: A woman literally uses her bare hands to bag coal for sale.

Right: With finely tuned balance, a cane basket seller rides out towards the countryside.

Far Right: Loaded down with her wares, a woman pushes her cycle while hoping for a sale.

Below: A cyclo passenger finds her shared load so comfortable it produces a yawn.

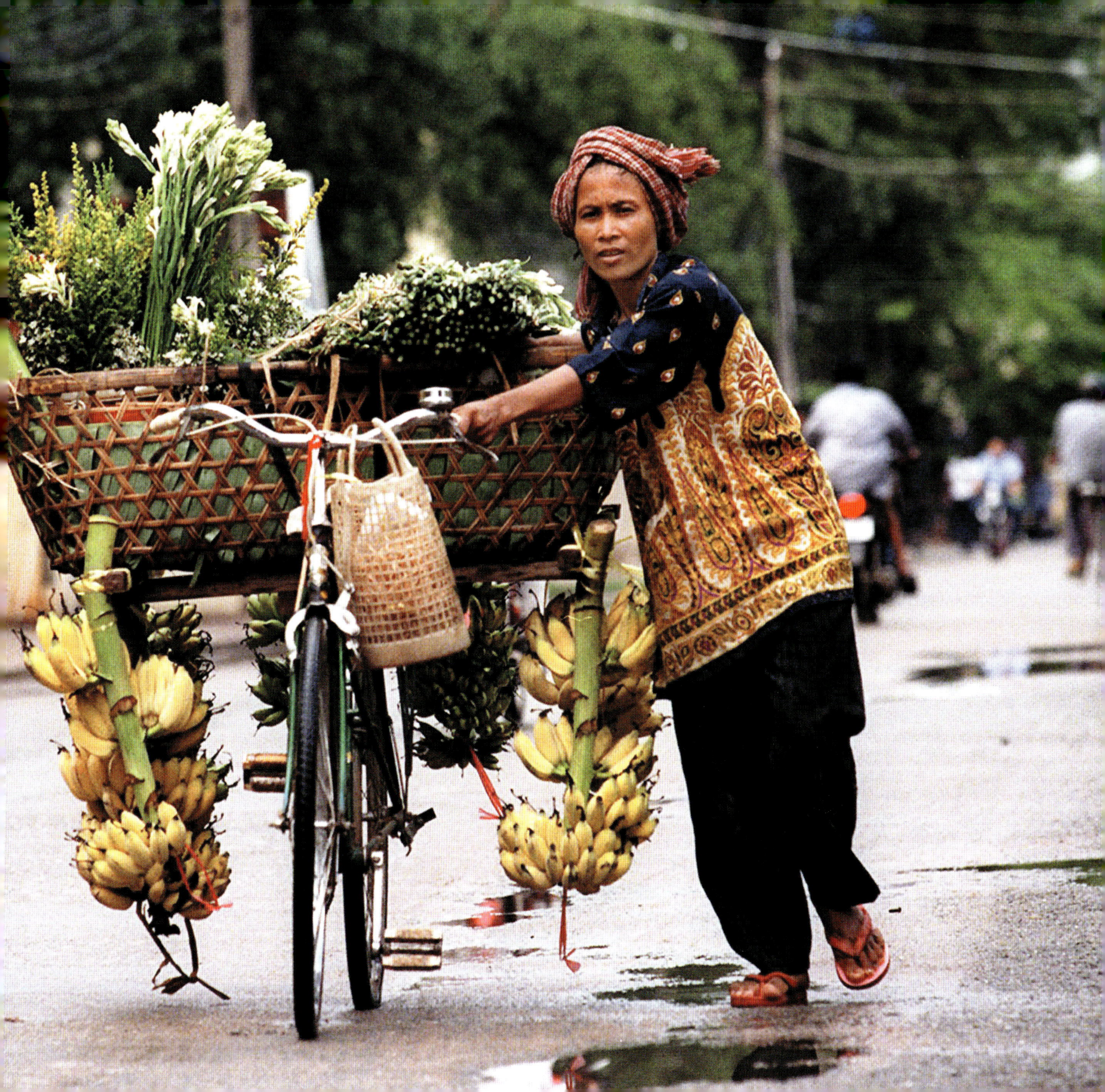

Starting work at an all too young age, a small girl looks for potential customers to sell her balloons.

A child sleeps under a mobile vendor's soft drink trolley.

Top: Wearing an impromptu wig, a woman walks the streets selling floor mats.

Above: A roadside stallholder puts her vibrantly colored sausages out on sale.

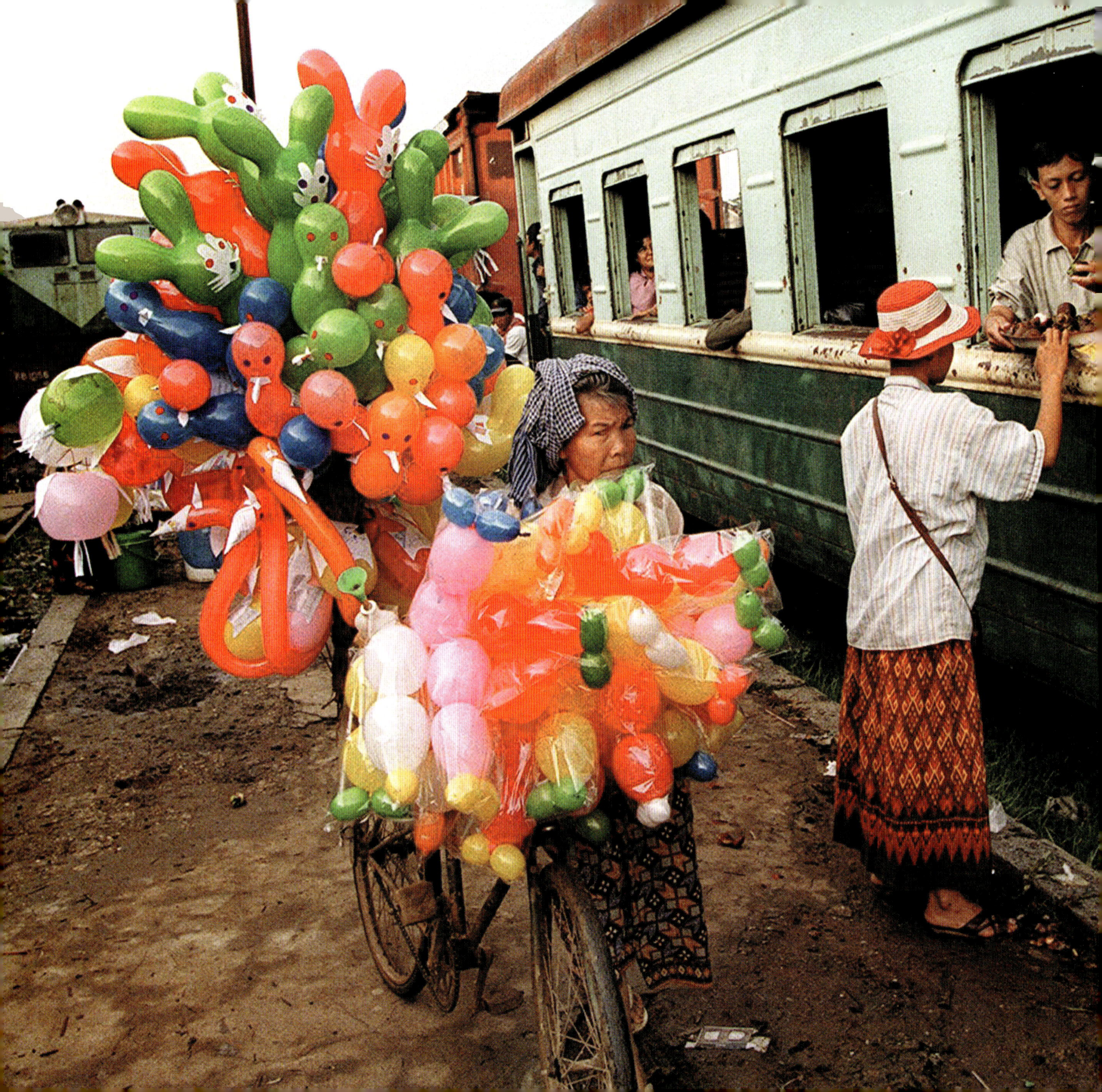

A colorful bunch of hawkers try selling their goods to passengers on a train from Battambang in the north of Cambodia.

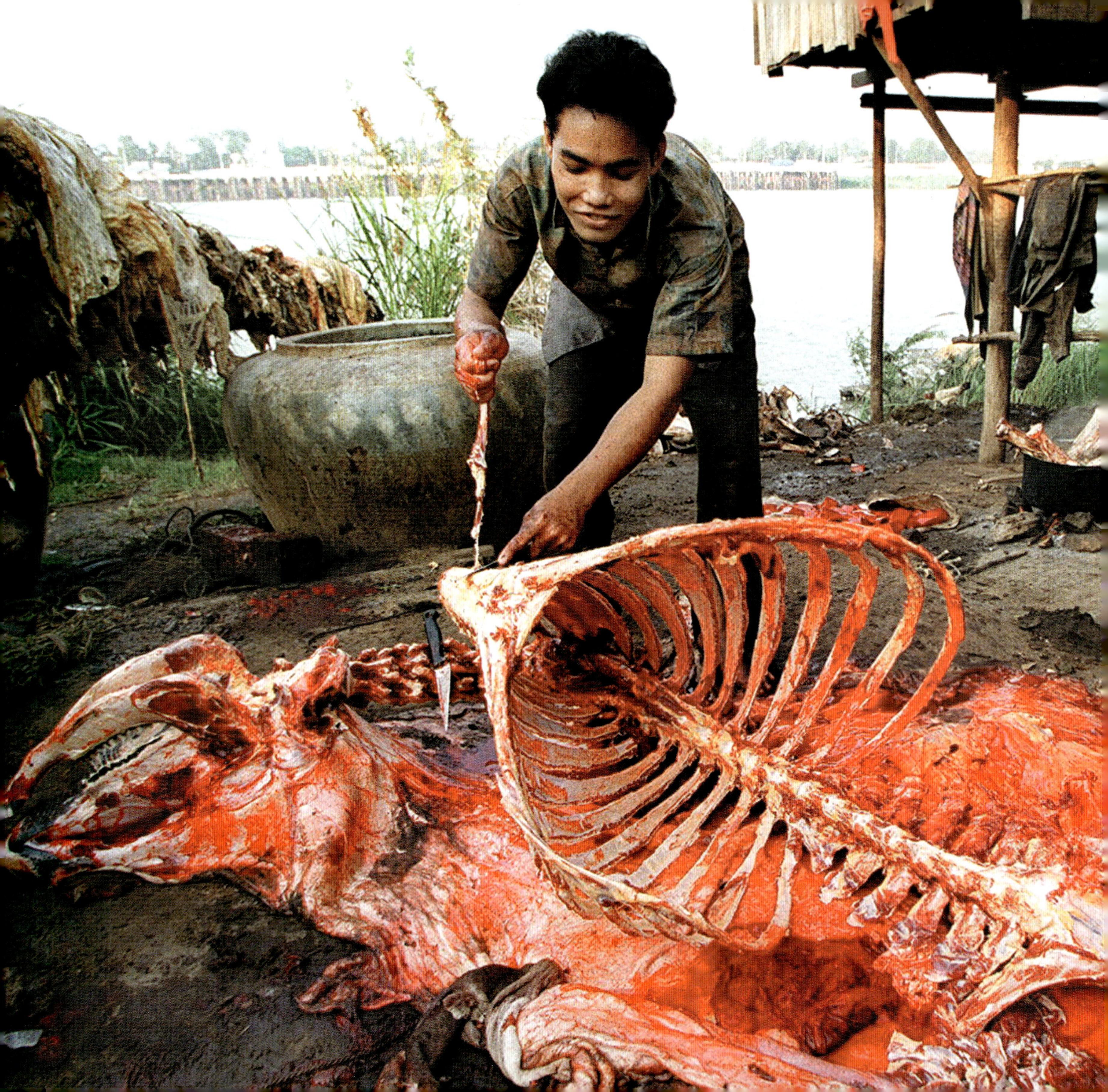

Top: A sun bear enjoys a respite from the hot sun, if not his chains.

Above: A stuffed bear, killed for its meat, strikes a fierce, if not ridiculous, pose.

Left: Not wanting anything to go to waste, a self-taught butcher strips clean the carcass of a beast.

93

Above: Early morning sees a rush to get freshly caught fish to the markets.

Right: Women sort through their net hoping there is enough to feed their families.

Following pages: The varied faces of Cambodia's fish processing industry.

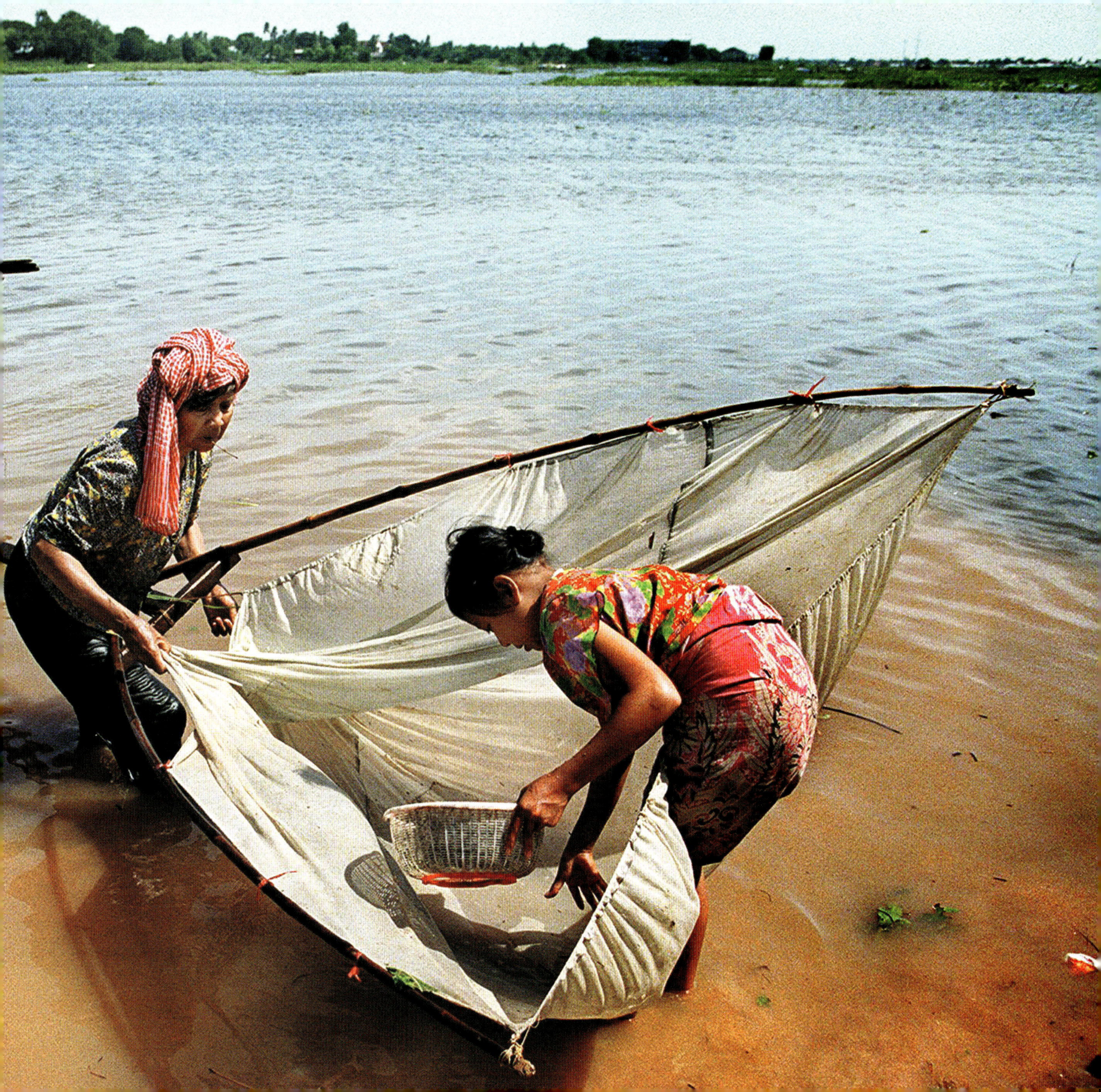

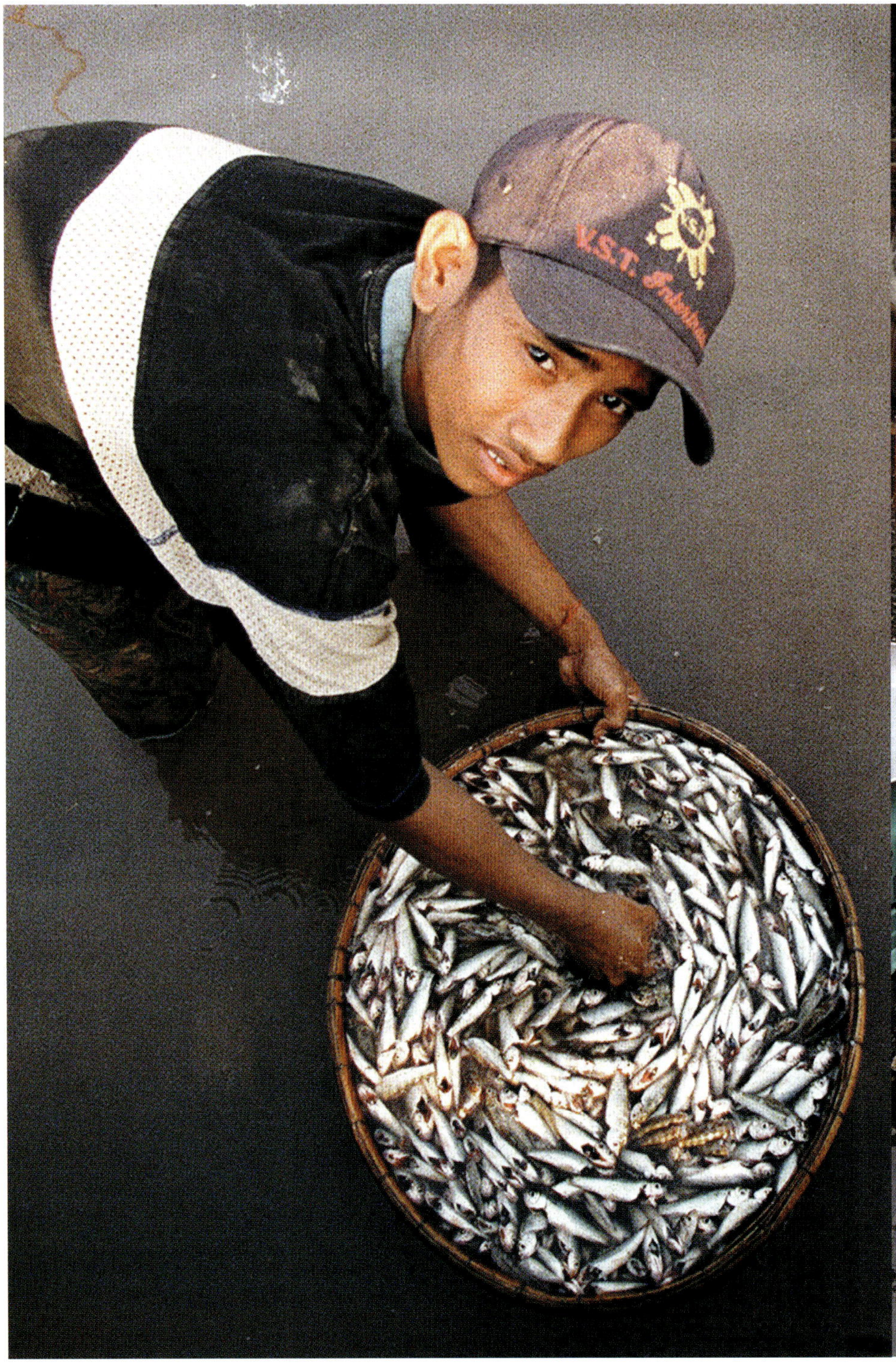
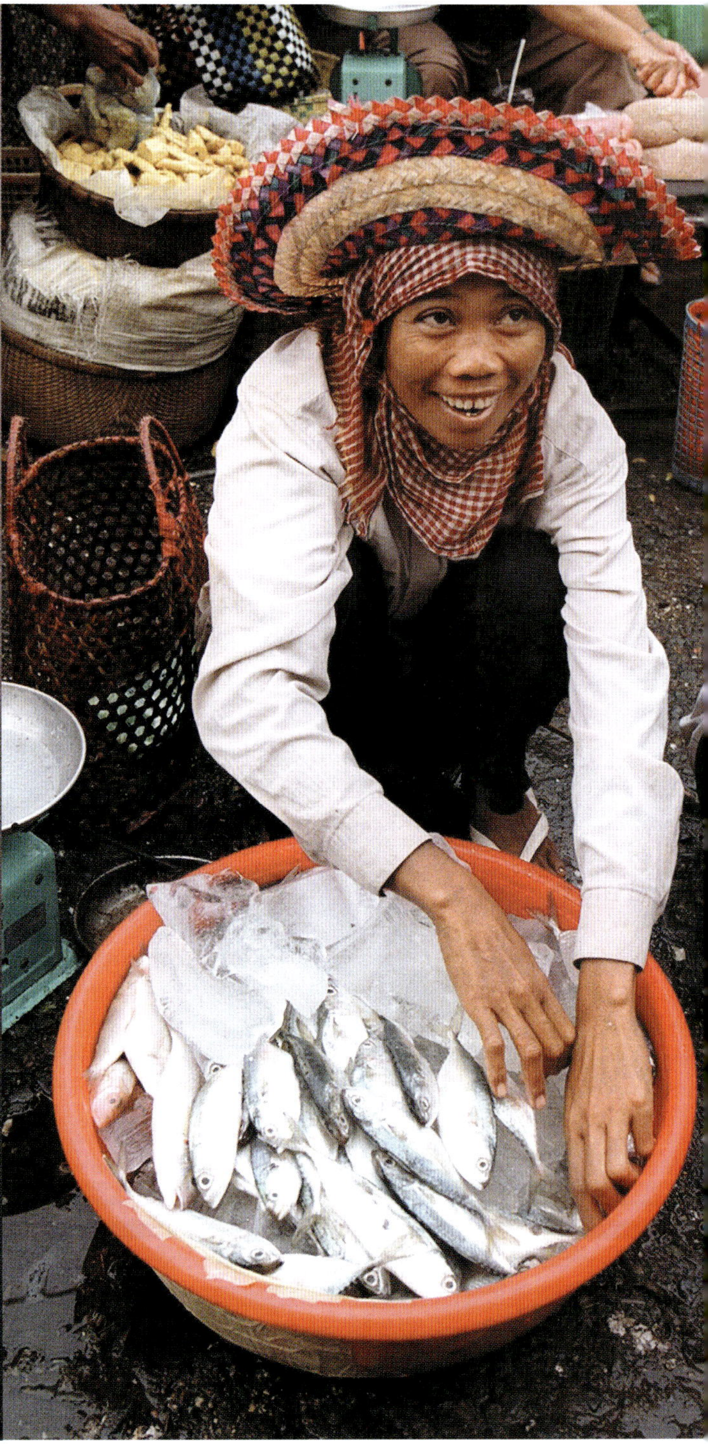

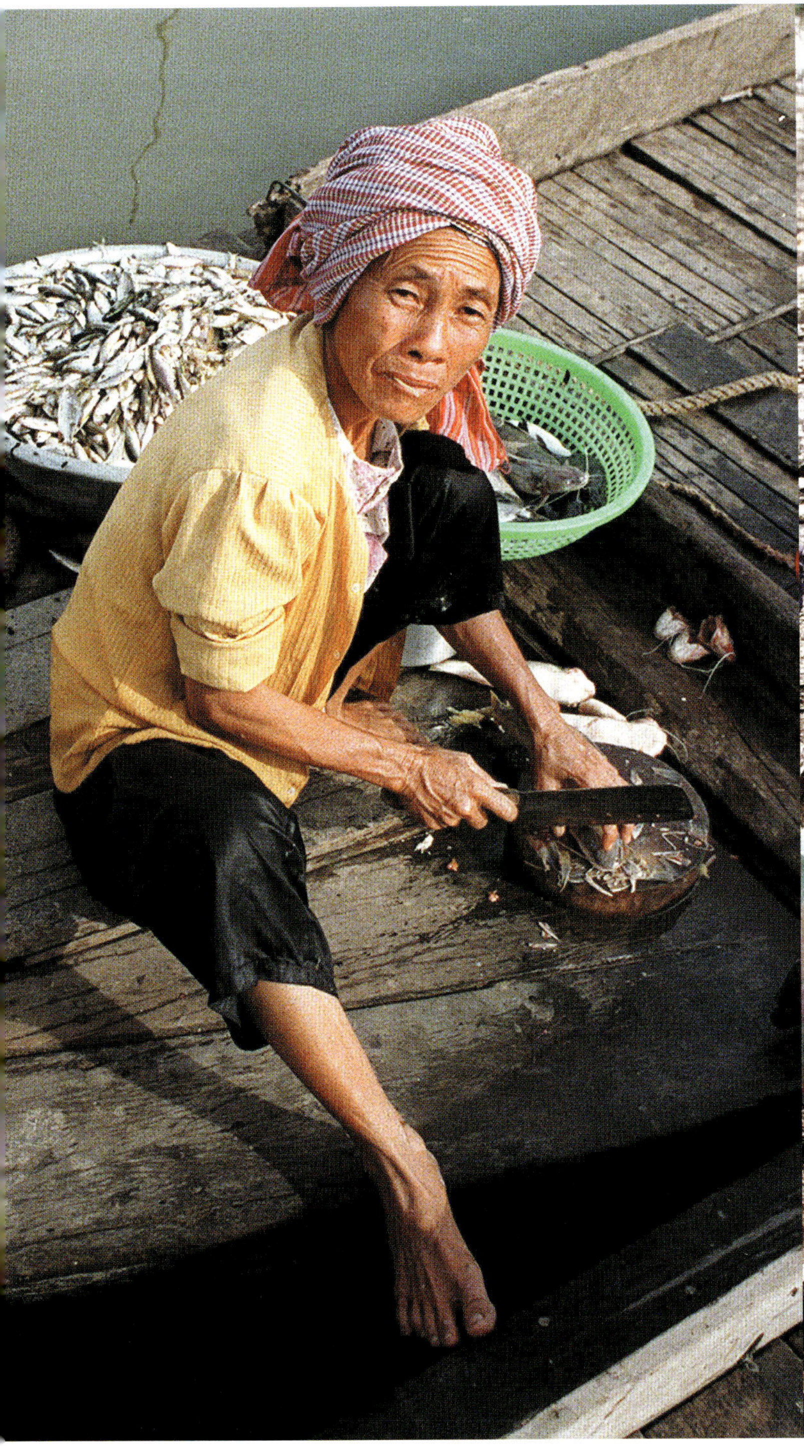
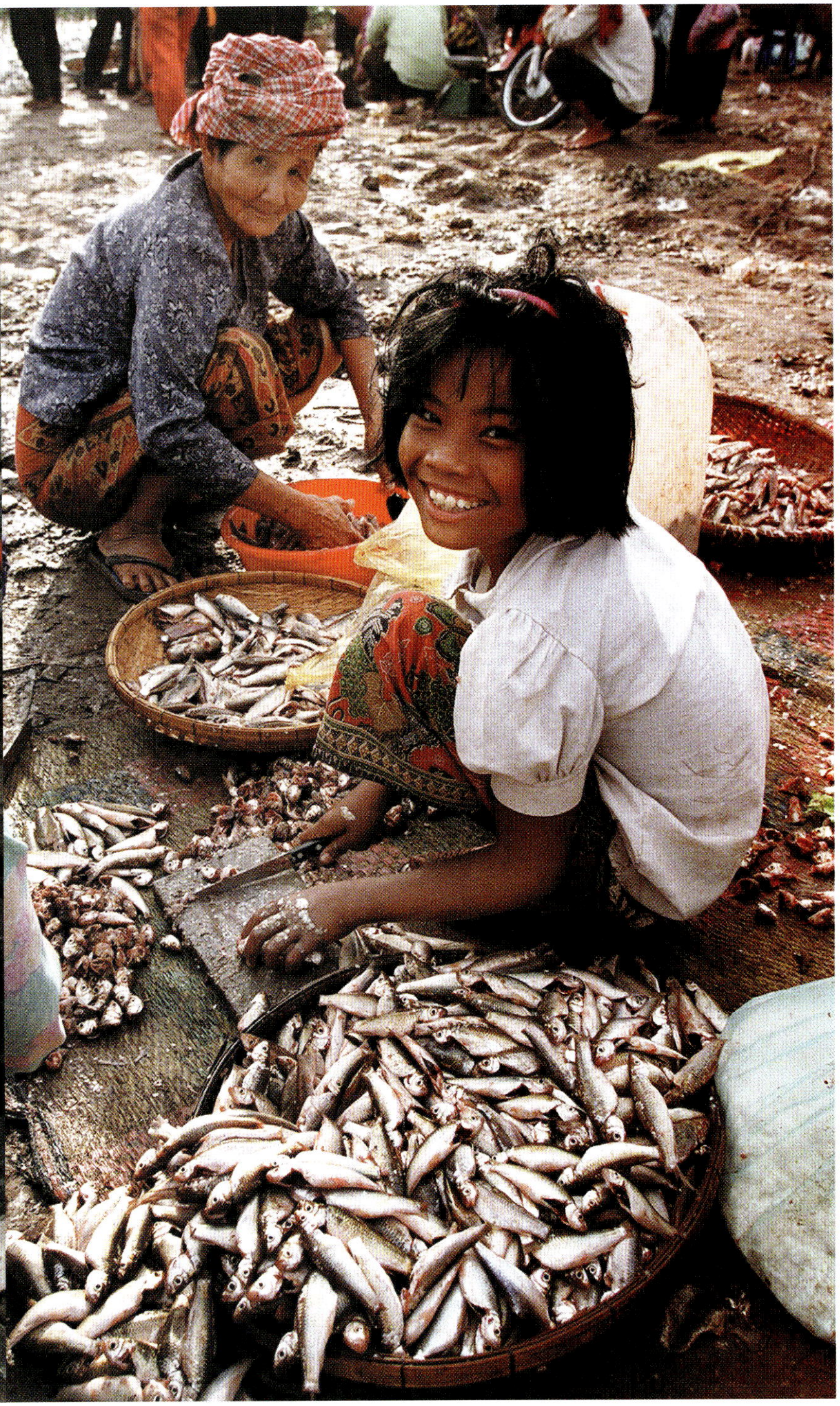

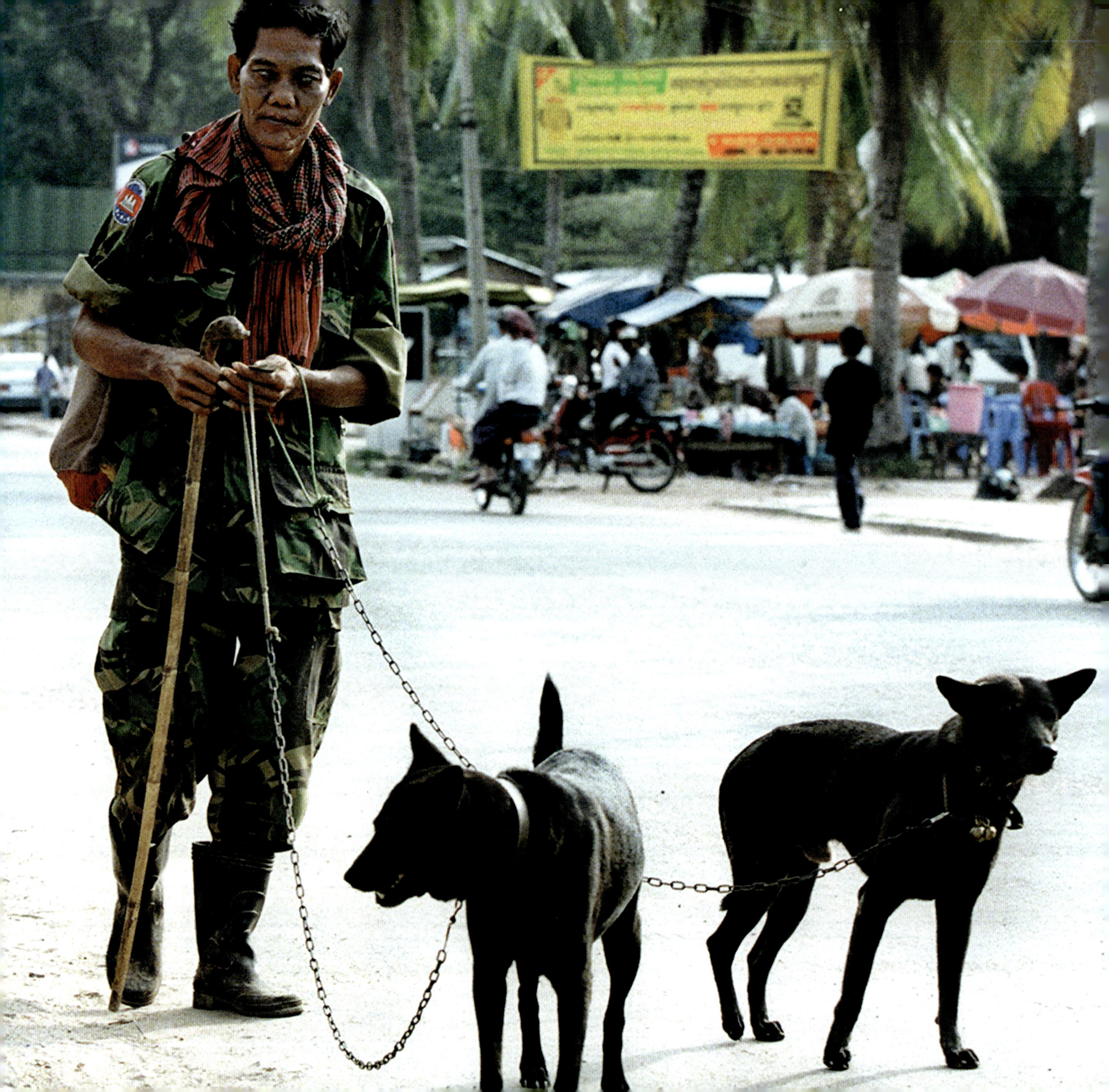

ON THE STREETS

Above: Rays of light break through overhead foliage as mottos make their way down a Phnom Penh street.

Left: Two dogs wander ahead of their blind owner as they walk the capital looking for handouts.

In an effort to clean up the country, particularly the capital Phnom Penh, after the extensive destruction from the Khmer Rouge era and subsequent civil war, the government and aid donors have injected millions of dollars into a beautification program. Renovations and new building construction are on the increase, as well as the resurfacing and maintenance of existing roads, but take a tour outside the cities and you'll soon be bogged down in mud in the wet season, or have your bones shaken during the dry.

On the busy city center streets, especially in the capital, business appears to be booming, and lifestyles that were once destroyed and stolen before people's very eyes are on the rebound. From designer-brand high-class fashion shops on the main thoroughfares, to hawkers along the side of roads, everyone is out there trying to make a living. Former communists may be in charge, but this is capitalism at its purest.

A visit to the markets gives an insight into the diverse culture of the Khmer people — abundantly alive with character and color. At a small market in the capital, only a block away from the Tonle Sap flood plain, elderly women with weathered faces sit side by side with their cane baskets full of dew-fresh produce; smiling to would-be customers, they expose their red-colored, betel nut stained teeth. Small children squat and form lines at the entrance to the market, usually selling small fish and little bundles of herbs displayed in shallow cane baskets strategically balanced on their heads.

Larger fish flip and flap in a desperate attempt for freedom, minutes before losing their heads to the chopper. Meat hangs on hooks, and displayed pig heads take pride of place. Frogs and snakes also feature when in season, while hairy barbecued spiders are considered delicacies.

A one-legged beggar sits in the street hoping that a passerby will take pity on his plight.

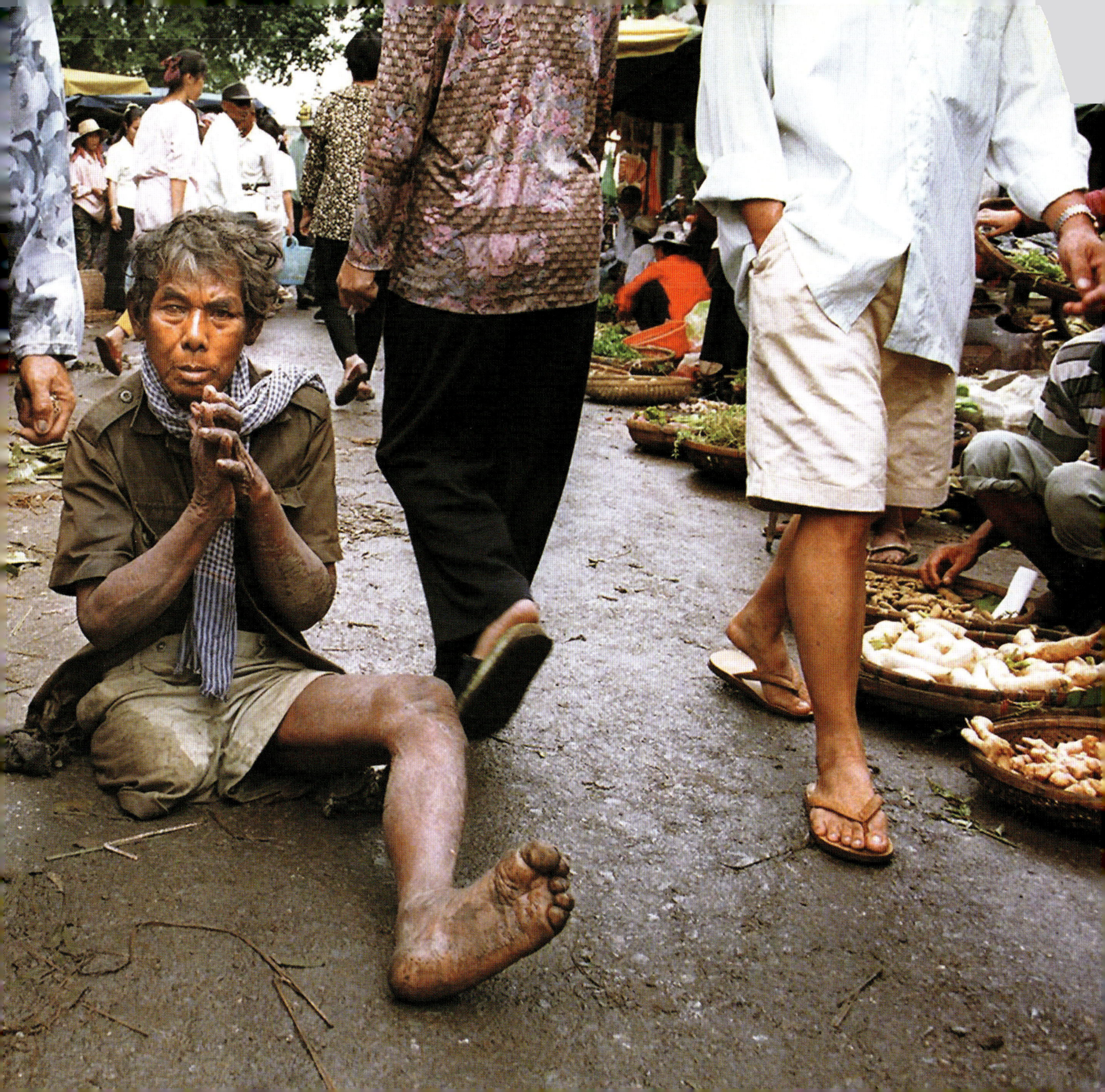

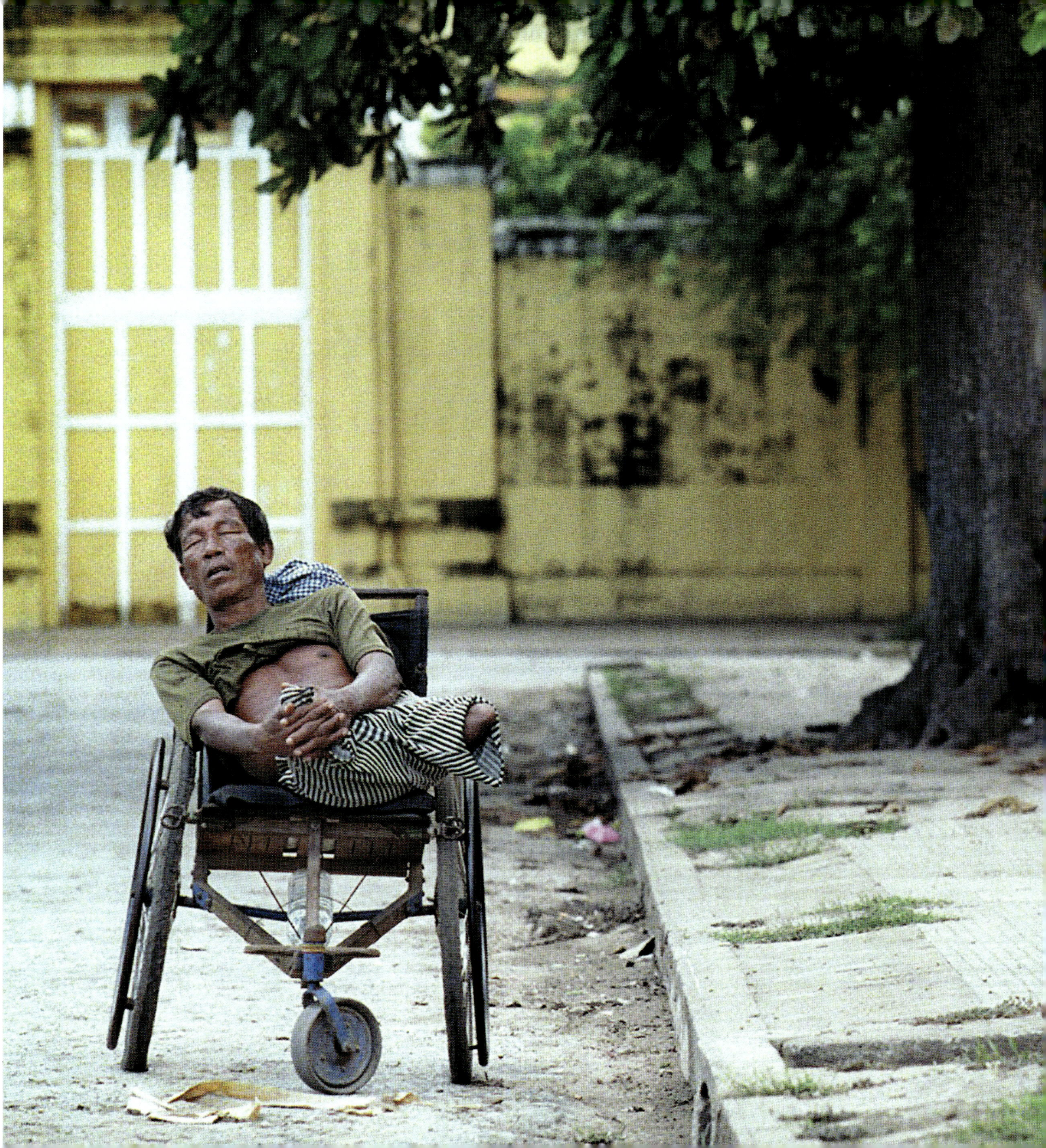

A passing monk steals a glance at a land mine victim asleep in his wheelchair.

Above: A group of children rummage through a pile of garbage for slender pickings.

Right: A pair of twins appear to be protecting their blind mother as the family of three beg on the city streets.

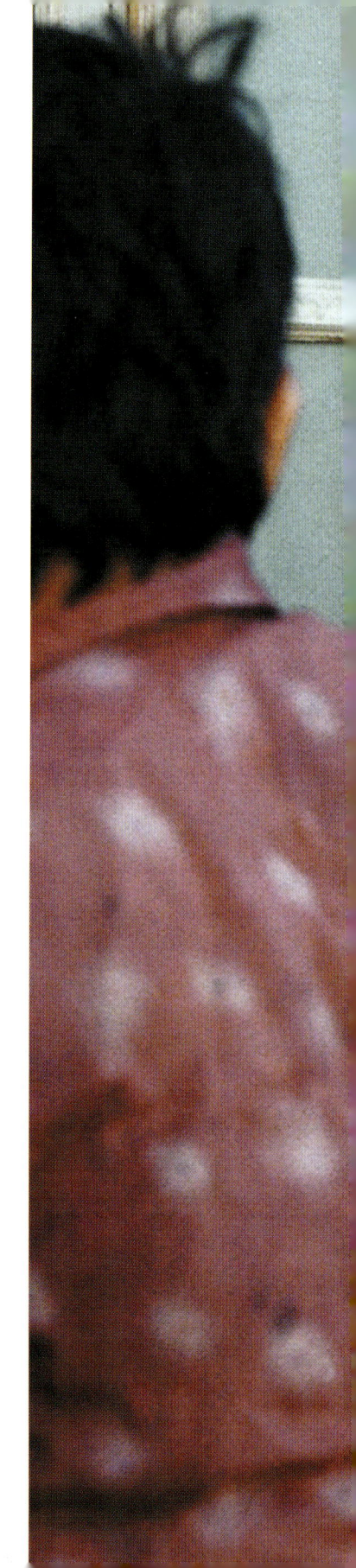

104

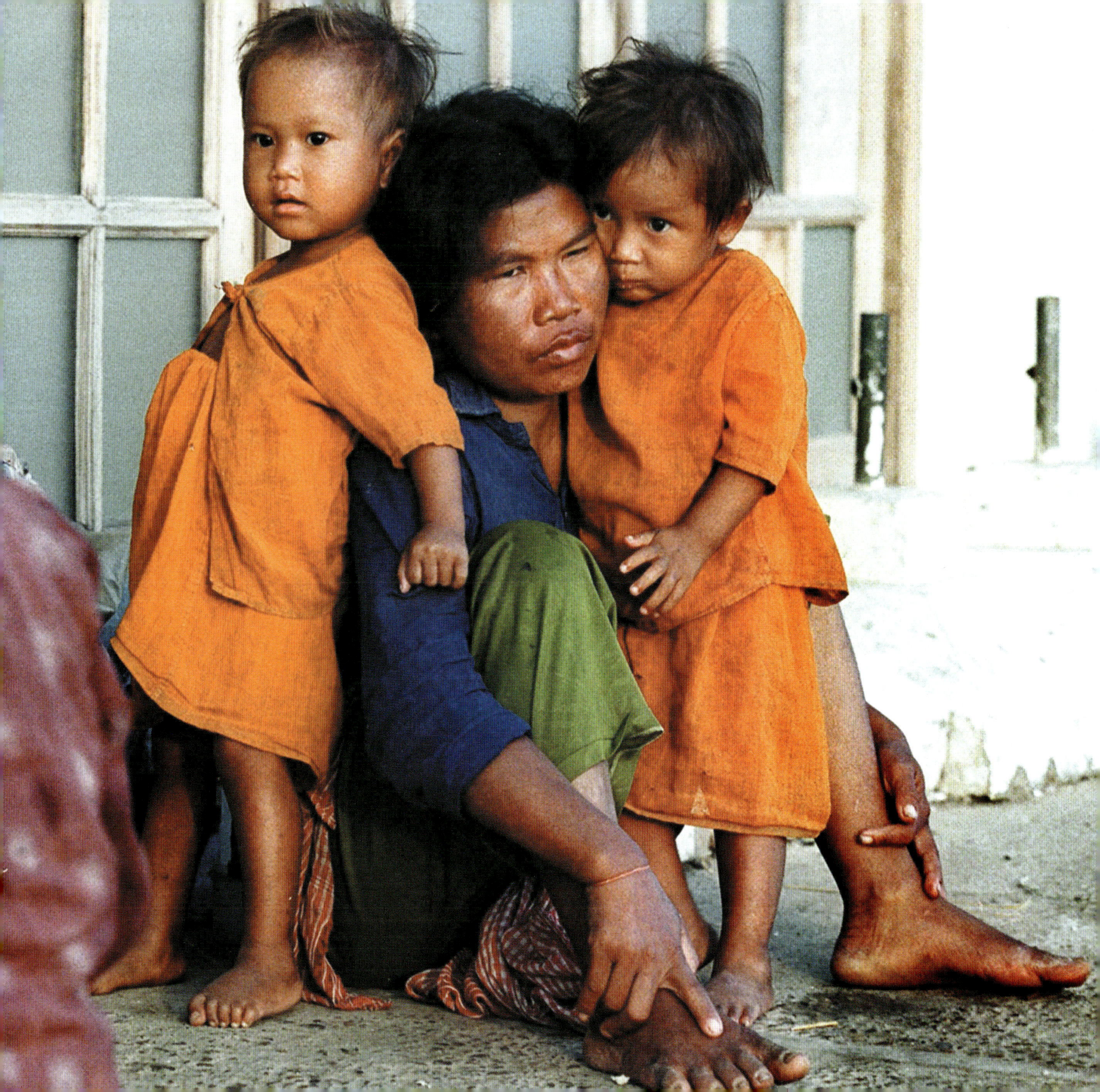

Boy's best friend?— a youngster takes his monkey for a walk on the city streets.

106

Street children watch transfixed as a performing chained monkey takes a hard earned meal break.

Looking out for anything remotely salvageable to put in their bags, scavenger children walk the streets.

Weighed down with his load, a boy makes his way across a city street with his bread.

109

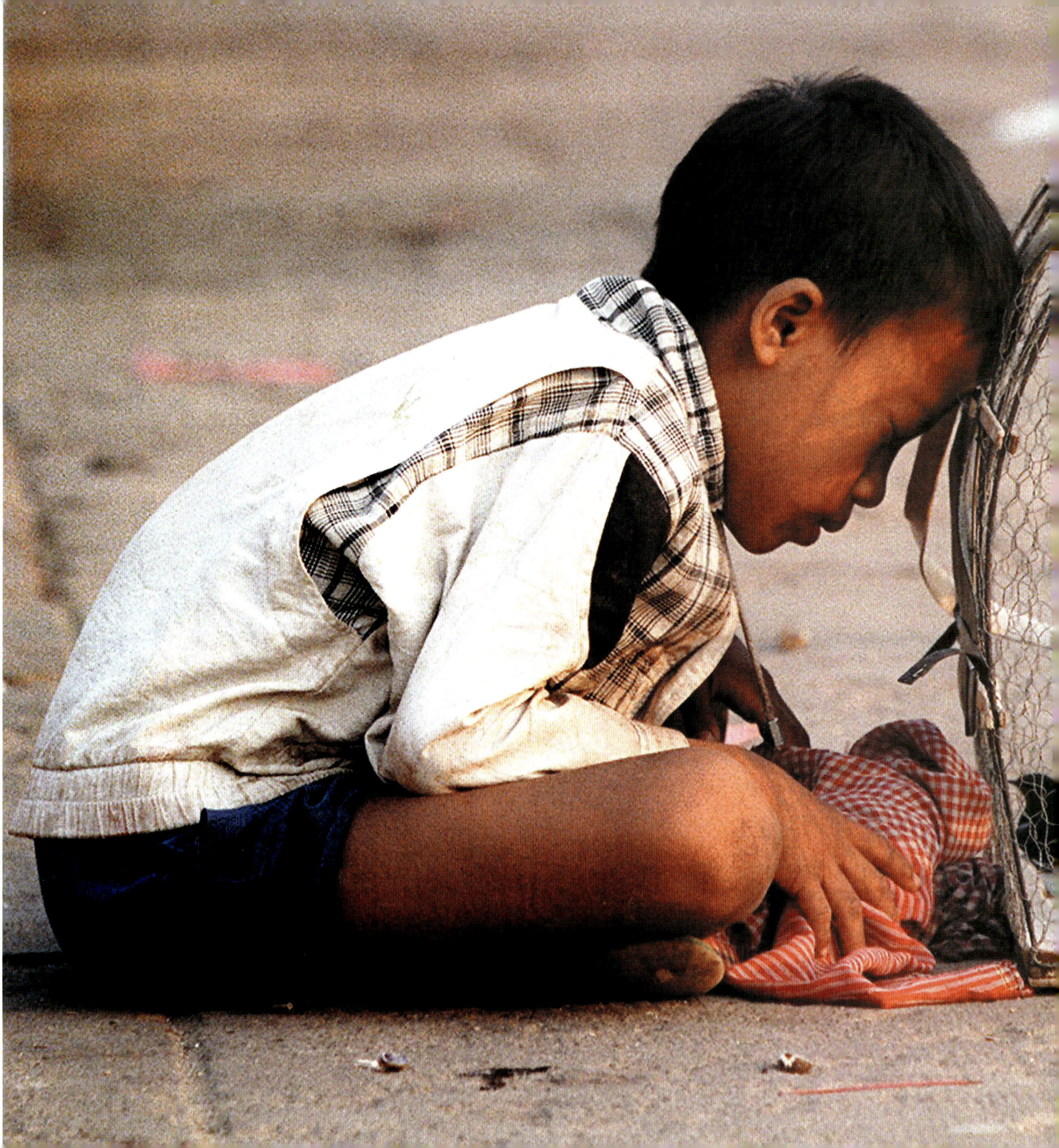

*Trapped in his own confines of poverty,
a young boy slumps in exhaustion against the
cage of birds he attempts to sell every day.*

Right: Rain or shine, city hawkers ply their trade regardless of the weather.

Far right: Two boys riding a bicycle share an umbrella for protection.

Below: Struggling to keep dry under a plastic sheet, cyclo passengers huddle together.

Below right: Motto riders share more than a ride during a rainstorm.

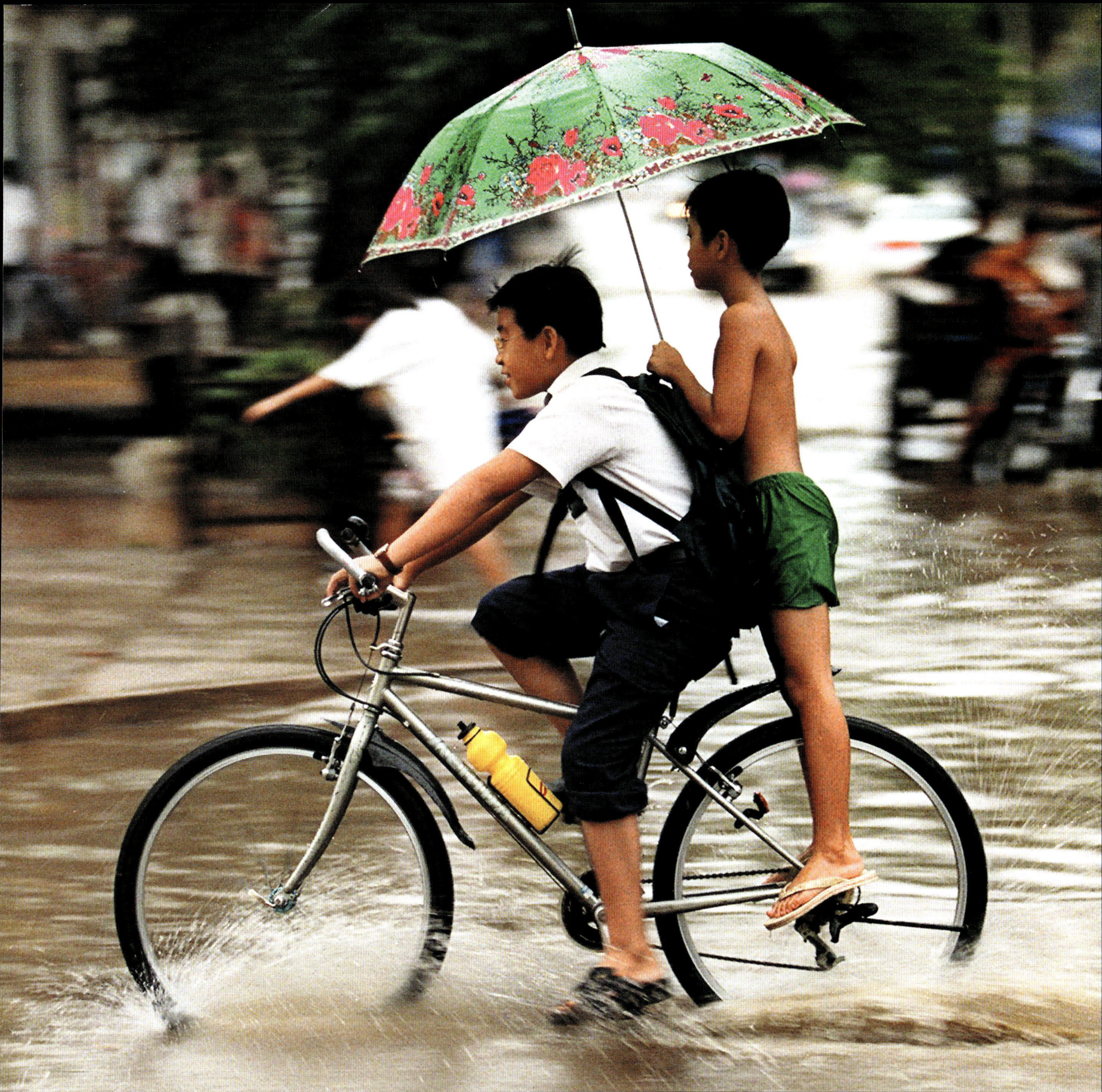

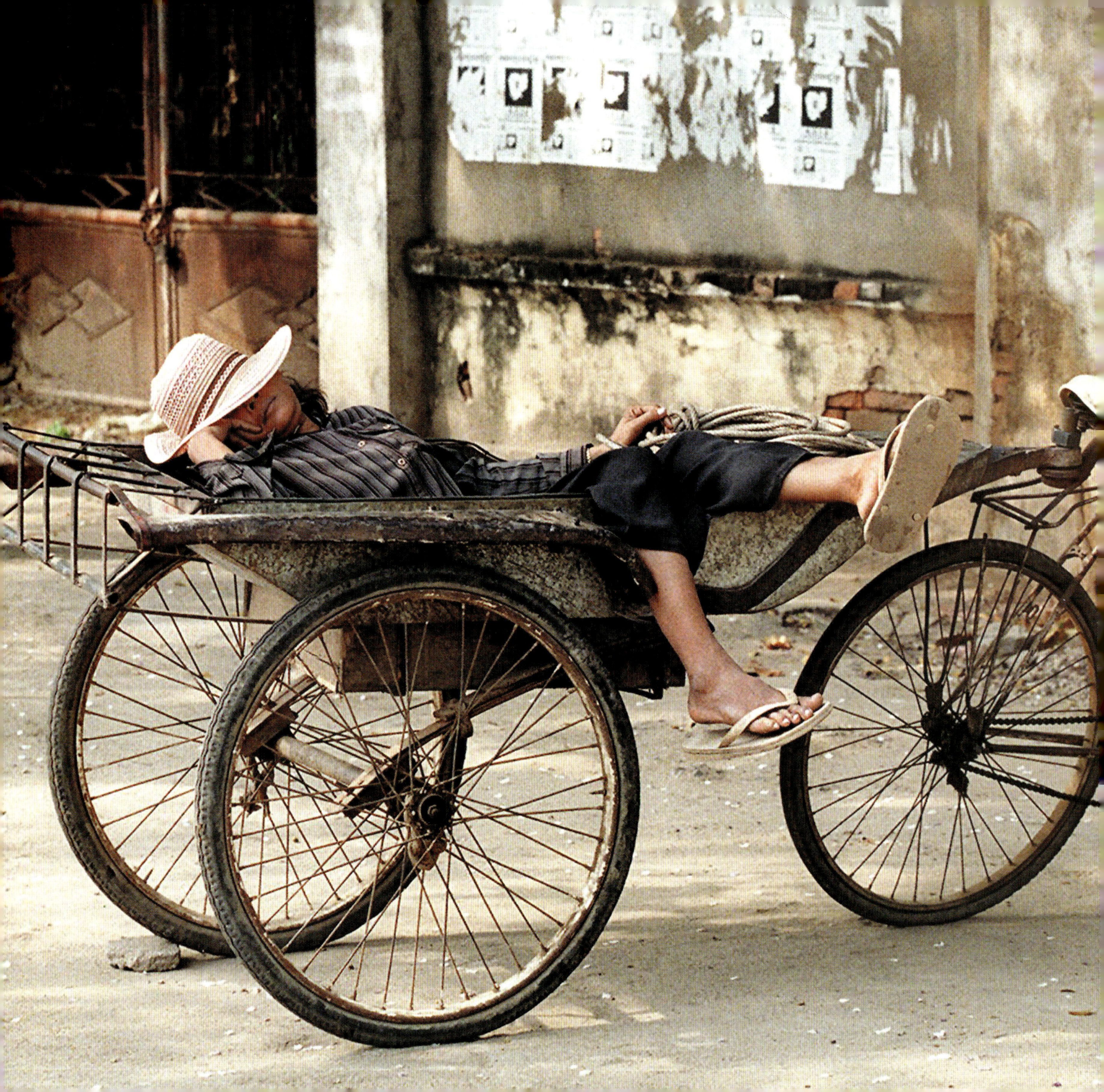

Top: A motto driver uses his bike to grab a quick nap.

Above: A cyclo driver uses a tree to put his feet up as he enjoys an afternoon sleep.

Left: A coconut seller takes a rest on the back of his cart.

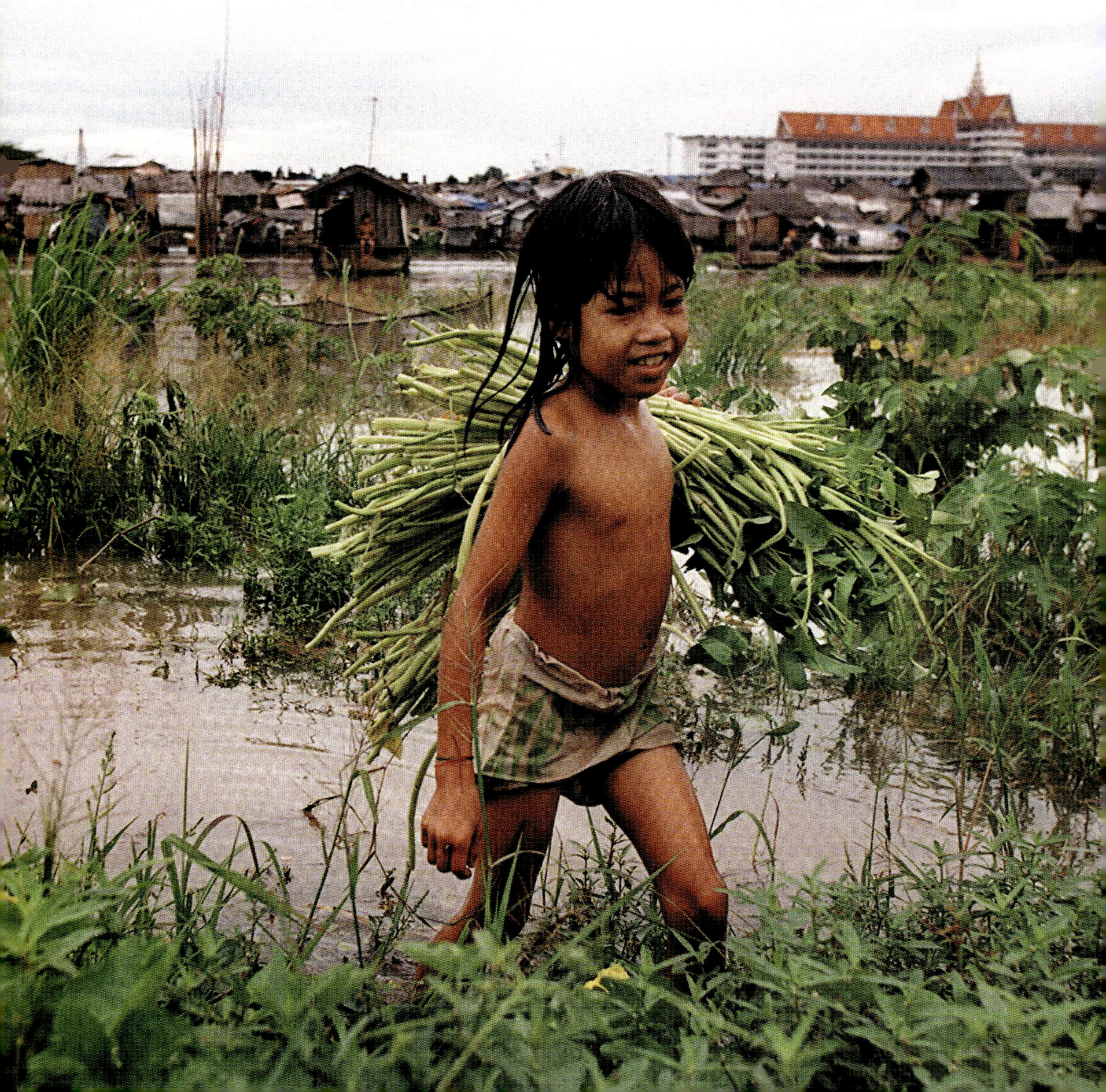

THE FUTURE

So where is Cambodia going? It has an aid-dependent economy, limited natural resources, and a burgeoning youth eager to enjoy the fruits of a lifestyle they see next door in Thailand, or beamed to them through foreign media. It has an ailing king, a fragile government, and a tenuous position perched between two of Southeast Asia's more powerful states — Thailand and Vietnam. In the countryside are millions of land mines, foreign investors are wary of having their fingers burnt again, and the infrastructure of roads can only be described as bone-crunching.

The end of the Cold War may have provided a breath of peace, but it has been a double-edged sword. With Cambodia no longer figuring highly on the geo-strategic map, the greatest danger now is a curse of "donor fatigue" that would see crucial handouts directed to the world's more pressing trouble spots. The pockets of foreign donors do have a limit, and Cambodia is being asked to stand on its own feet.

The country is cautiously stepping in that direction, nervously placing itself in the Southeast Asian regional community, while keeping its ties to former colonial masters intact. English, and not French, is now the second language of choice. Telecommunications to the outside world, once limited to a few lines via Moscow, is a booming industry. For those rich enough, there is also the Internet.

But the blunt reality is that Cambodia has been, and still is, a hostage to its outside environment. Its fortunes are inextricably linked to global forces and pressures outside its control. Internally, it has a people suffering a collective trauma, and a power structure that, in the recent past, brutally demonstrated its ability to collapse at any given moment. What is clear is that every player is trying to make up for lost time, and while the country may not be heading for greatness, it may be at last heading for peace.

Above: Street children raid a garbage bin hunting for food, only to find an unappetizing toothbrush.

Left: A young girl seems happy with her task of finding water plants to sell at the market.

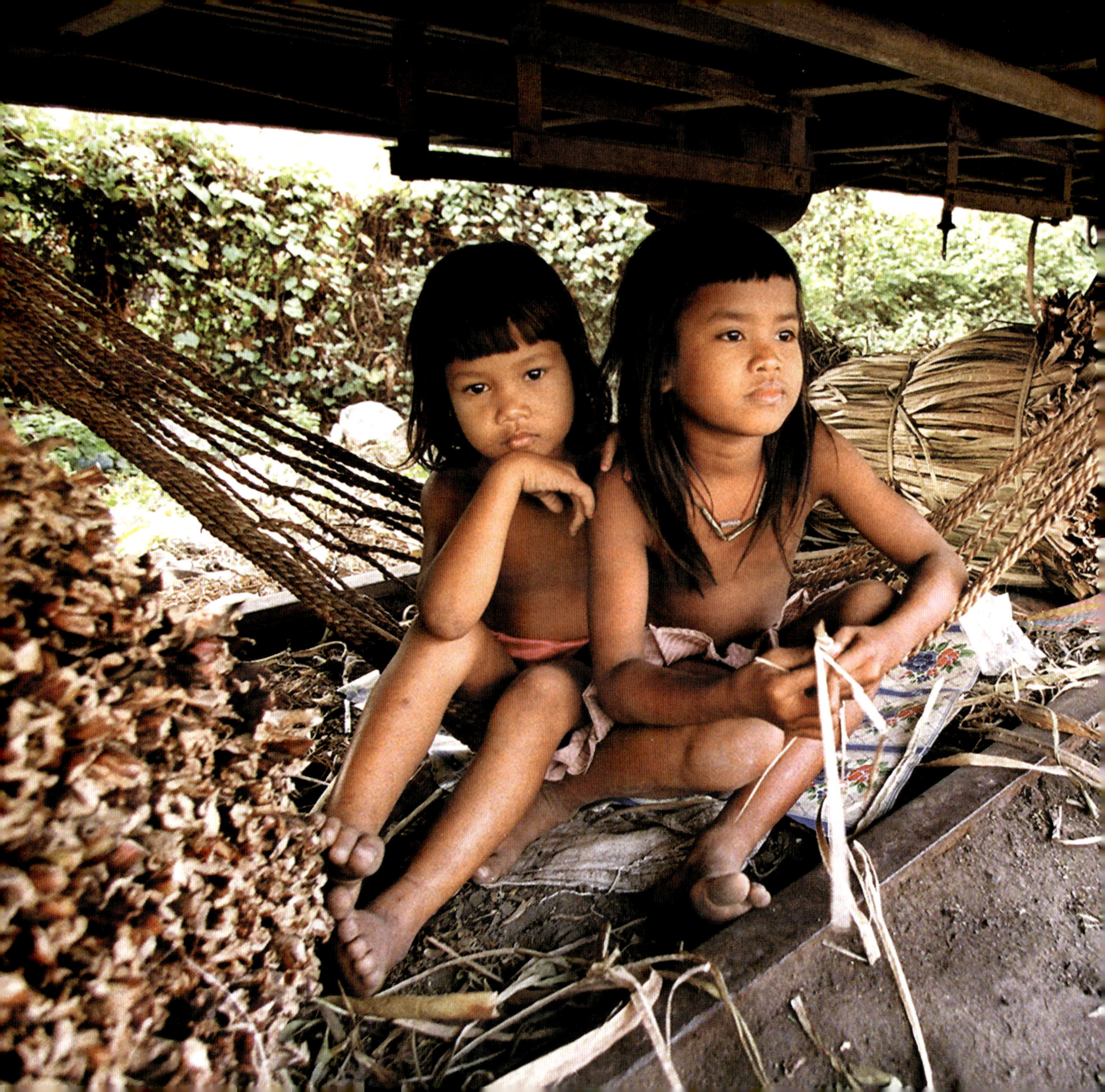

Left: An AIDS infected orphan waits in hope for someone to take an interest.

Far left: Two girls wake from sleeping in their makeshift bed — a hammock slung underneath a train carriage.

Below: Two children smile happily, completely unaware they have AIDS and are orphans.

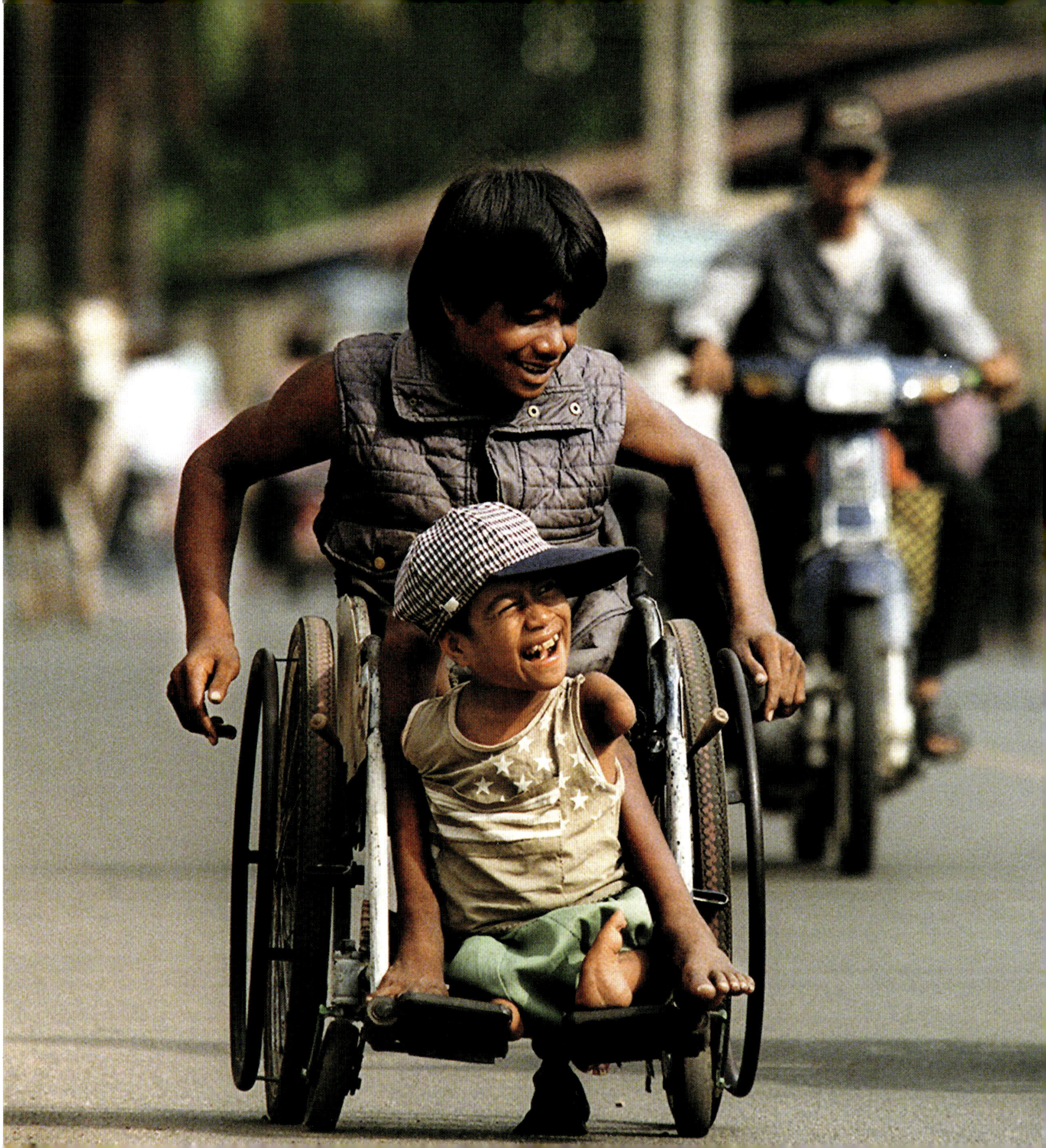

Above: Layered precariously, this group ignore the dangers and enjoy the thrills as they speed down the highway.

Left: Two boys briefly escape their disabilities as they enjoy the freedom and mobility provided by a wheelchair.

121

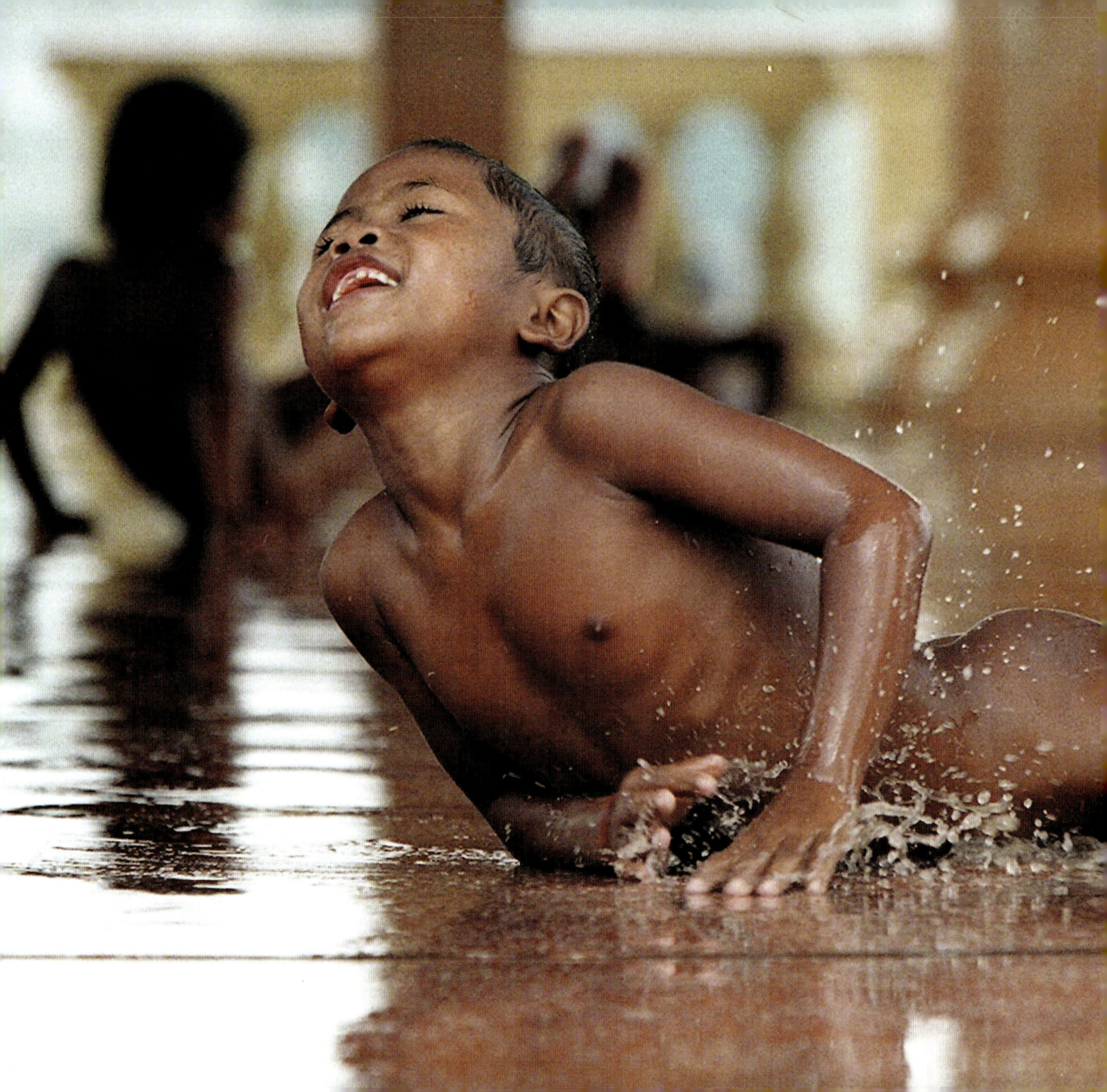

Top: Children cheekily impersonate the photographer taking their portraits.

Above: Children have the time of their lives playing in the mud on the banks of the Mekong River.

Left: A boy makes his own fun sliding on the wet tiles at a pagoda.

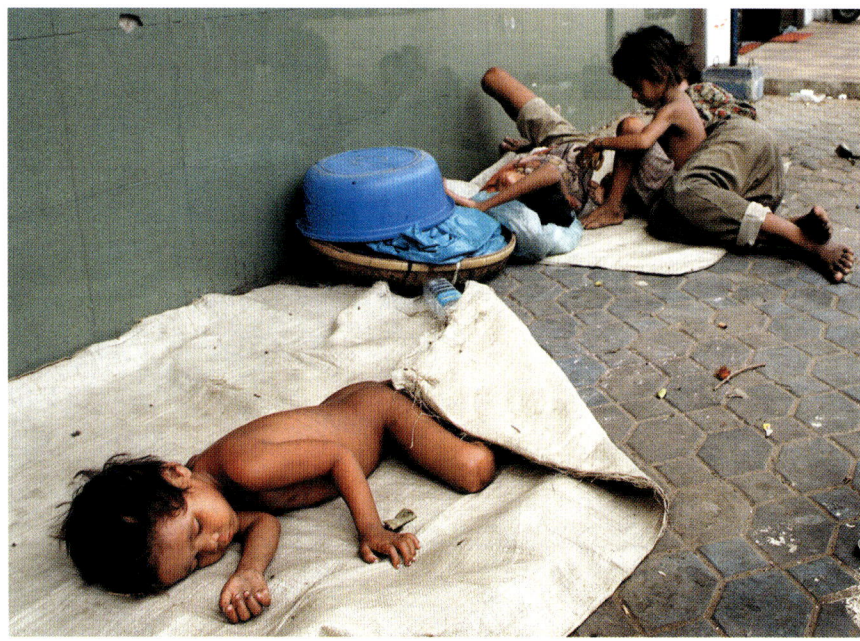

Top: Fishing village children are happy enough playing soccer with a deflated ball.
Above: Children sleep rough on the streets of Phnom Penh.
Right: Street children lounge about in their father's cart at a place they call home.

Top: A girl selling food waits expectantly for the boats to come in and her customers to arrive.

Above: With her dog seemingly scouting ahead for obstacles, a young girl maneuvers her wooden boat at a fishing village north of Phnom Penh.

Left: A girl protectively holds a young goat from the herd that she is minding.

A goat receives a human helping hand to find some food.